SIMON TOBIN

Tales From The Big Yellow

Unreliable Memoirs of a Tour Guide

For Jake
And in memory of Paolo Fortini

When I was younger I could remember anything, whether it happened or not.

Mark Twain

Contents

1

Beginnings

Sultans of Swing echoed from the tape deck as we drove down towards the coast of Montenegro, jostling together as our van took the tight corners. Below us, like cocaine lines upon a mirror, we could see the streams of white water behind the ferries crossing the Gulf of Kotor. Blue sky framed the rocky hillside that angled upwards from the water's edge. Tall pines clung on, throwing fingers of shade over spreads of yellow gorse. It was warm with just enough breeze to stir the wispy grass and give uplift to the buzzards circling above.

Then it happened. A deep rumble, the trees and ground began to shake.

With a sudden, stomach-churning lurch, our vehicle plunged into the brown blur exploding towards us. The ear-splitting noise faded into silence, followed by a yawing metallic sound. Thick dust swirled everywhere.

'Holy shit!'

'What happened? Is everyone alright?'

'I'm okay, I think,' spitting dust from my mouth.

'Must have been an earthquake.'

'Or a bomb.'

'Hang on, let's get sorted and out of this mess.' It was DDH's voice. 'Is everyone okay?'

'Yeah.'

'Not sure.'

'Hold it. Get organized. Call out your names.'

The roll call complete, we pulled ourselves from the wreck. The procedure wasn't easy. The van, a VW coaster with 16 seats, had fallen into a jagged-edged ditch some ten feet deep where the tarmac road had sheared apart in the sudden earthquake. It was as if an underground force had rent upwards, splitting the landscape in two, and then a giant hand had peeled back the road, like folding back a sardine tin, with our vehicle the lone fish.

We collected ourselves beside a demolished pine, inspected our wounds and took stock.

'Fucking nearly died.' Scraps' Aussie drawl cut across our stunned silence.

I looked along the line of twelve guys, sitting or leaning with backs against the fallen tree trunk. Everyone was covered in brown dust. Heads down, almost remorsefully, as if we'd had a manic fight with pillows filled with dust rather than feathers.

Miraculously no-one was badly injured. Muff, we discovered, had fractured his arm and Shirl, the big Kiwi realized, about an hour later, that he had dislocated two fingers. Everyone was grazed, cut and bruised. My worst injury was a bite in my tongue. Gushing blood made it look a lot worse than it was.

Slowly, with heads clearing and DDH leading the discussion, we set about deciding what we should do. Our transport was smashed to pieces, we were probably 15 kilometers from the Kotor chain ferry, which from our lofty location, was a tiny white dot on the shoreline below. The road ahead and behind us was such a mess that no rescue vehicle, other than a helicopter, would make it to us for days. There was no alternative but to walk.

We formed an impromptu chain gang and handballed bags and belongings from the wreckage.

'Up there Cazaly,' Scraps cried, and we set off downhill, twelve stragglers clutching hold-alls, sleeping bags and, except for DDH, a briefcase each.

It must have been a bizarre sight. It was February 1979.

The journey that led us to that Montenegran hillside began on January 4th of that year, on a cold miserable morning in Rathbone Place, London.

Eleven brand-new briefcases were lined up in a shop doorway avoiding the rain, and the VW van was parked at an angle on the pavement. A few of our group were loading bags, whilst others were stubbing out the odd cigarette or laughing nervously, hands thrust in pockets for confidence.

Our leader sat taciturn in the driver's seat.

'Get on with it, you Marys, we've a ferry to catch,' DDH said in his dry Kiwi tone. In the weeks to come, we'd find it could be reassuring, even warm, but mostly it was a sarcastic barb that would unerringly find its mark.

We were new recruits and it was DDH's role to train us as tour guides who would lead coach tours around Europe. Many of our group had travelled in Africa, Asia and overland from London to Kathmandu but few knew Europe well.

This intense training trip would tell us all we'd need to know as Tour Guides. What we could not know at the time was that the friendships forged within this group and the characters we would meet en route would influence our lives and careers for years to come.

Our group of trainee tour guides consisted of Aussies and Kiwis, except for me, the token Pom. A chain of coincidences had led me from a brief role as a Drama teacher in England, through a year as a kayak instructor in France followed by extensive travelling, to finally answering an advert in a free London paper for "Young adventurous types to lead groups of young people in Europe and beyond."

Mentally toughened from previous travels with Antipodeans, I could handle my fair share of ribbing or "Pommie-bashing" which began as soon as we met. There were the usual references to our weakness at sport, our lack of personal hygiene, our "piss weak" showers and our propensity to whinge. I retorted by questioning the general lack of Australian culture, intellect or spirituality.

'You mean we're big and empty like our country?' Scraps exchanged good-naturedly as we shared beers the night before the off. 'Good on yer.'

The relaxed and friendly nature of my Aussie and Kiwi companions made it easy to make friends and we eleven recruits established a genuine mateship immediately.

I should explain at this point that the antipodean term "mate" does not refer to or imply a partner in procreation. A "mate" is rather usually male and implies an egalitarian acceptance; a level in common; a confidante; an unquestioning support at all times. Your true, real mate is there for you when everyone else has deserted you and at your lowest ebb will offer genuine support, such as 'Get on with it, you fuckwit!'

Furthermore, Aussies and Kiwis use nicknames to enhance the intimacy of a developed mateship. Sometimes an abbreviation is used. My nickname for example became, and remains to this day, "Tobes". On the other hand, a nickname can reflect a particular predilection for something or for some activity; such as "Ladbroke" who was, not surprisingly, keen on betting. It can also be simply descriptive, such as "Shirl" whose big frame was topped with blonde curly hair, just like the child star Shirley Temple.

I will leave you to interpret the origin of the other nicknames in our group which were; "Scraps", "Spoof", "Daki", "Meeny", "The Director", "Muff", "Block of Flats" and "Wanker".

Later in this tale we may explore the difference between Tour Guides and Tour Drivers, who generally carry even more bizarre names; "Filthy Frank", "Sperm Whale", "Horse", "Rabbit" and "the Six-Foot Poof" are a few examples. At this point however, it is important to merely take note that there is always a basis upon which a nickname is founded, and the fact that eight hours after leaving London, by way of a ferry from Dover to Calais, we arrived in Paris and our adventure had begun.

I use the word "adventure" advisedly, because we were first and foremost on a training trip to equip us with the skills needed to qualify as Tour Guides. We would need knowledge, experience, "nouse", great interpersonal skills, leadership qualities, and an ability to make judgements in a tight spot. We'd also need thick skin and remarkable energy when leading tours of Europe for paying travellers, all aged from 18 to 35, who were keen to experience as much as possible on trips that ranged from 14 to a whopping 90 days.

And nothing more embodied the essence of this training and the associated learning process than that iconic European Tour Guiding experience, the Paris Night Tour.

2

The Paris Night Tour

'Put your tents up quickly. They turn the lights out at ten pm on this campsite,' said DDH, when we arrived. His nickname, by the way, was simply his initials. 'We'll grab a quick feed, then head in to the city centre for the night tour. Tobes and Shirl, you cook.'

Huddling together for warmth in a small shower block, in a campsite, in the dark, in January, eating tinned tomatoes and pasta boiled on a large calor burner, not to mention sleeping in a tent, was certainly not "la vie Parisienne" of my fantasies. I had hoped for brasseries, Bordeaux wine and boeuf bourguignon. Clearly, we were being trained with certain cost controls in mind.

'Right let's go.'

My reverie broken, we washed plates and pots unhygienically in freezing water and piled into the van. Then we fumbled in the dark for our briefcases, pulling out pens and notepads to take directions and make notes in our bibles, which were awkwardly balanced on our knees.

Ah, the "Bible"; the novice Tour Guide's survival kit. The Bible is a thick ring binder filled with notes, directions, contacts, phone numbers, itineraries, dos and don'ts, and emergency advice. In short, the Bible contains the sum of knowledge built up, and passed on, by Tour Guides over the years.

We had already had an introduction to our bibles, spending the journey from London to Paris, studying them while we practiced speaking to a microphone and memorised potted French history, trying to digest the information required for the Night Tour of Paris. Now, with DDH at the wheel, we drove out of the Bois de Boulogne campsite, heading towards the bright city lights.

From that moment our experience literally changed gear.

We hammered up Rue de la Grande Armée and at a storming pace drove straight into the maelstrom of traffic circling the Étoile roundabout, in the middle of which stood the Arc de Triomphe, glowing gold and bold against the glitter of Les Champs Elysées. Our heads twisted from side to side as DDH rattled off the sights and directions as he drove.

'Get all of this down,' he said. 'I am going to show you round once; five of you will then give a night tour. If anyone cocks up we'll go around again until it's right.'

We exited Étoile and steamed up Rue de Kléber, noting Moorish artwork and trying to remember what DDH had said about Baron Haussman's city plan and why the Tomb of the Unknown Soldier was there, why cars gave way to incoming vehicles and why the metro signs were designed in Art Deco style. Then Muff asked a question.

'DDH, can you stop for a minute? I've dropped my pencil and can't see it in the dark of the van.'

'Yes,' I joined in. 'While we're stopped can I go and find a loo as the pasta is not going to hang around for long.'

The van careered to the side of the road and DDH slammed on the brakes. Taking his hands deliberately from the wheel he turned slowly and looked at us one by one. The streetlights from outside cast an ethereal glow on his grim features. He was not happy.

'Right, you Marys, I am going to say this once only. I don't give a flying fuck about pencils and Pommy bowel movements. This is a training trip; it is not a fucking holiday. This is the toughest thing you will do in your lives. If you pass this test you will take responsibility for a very expensive big, yellow Mercedes coach and 50 people and you will lead them all over Europe to Istanbul and back, via everywhere. I am going to teach you everything you need to know to do that and you are going to learn it. If you don't, or you can't do it, I will drop you and your bags at the nearest railway station and you can piss off. So, from this moment on, you will be on time, be well prepared, won't lose your pencil and make sure you have a shit before you get in the van!' He paused to catch breath after this crescendo. 'Any questions?' There was a slight hint of saliva at the side of his mouth.

Whether it was a joint determination on our part, or the sheer force of DDH's imposing will, we all nodded. Block, short for "Block of Flats", a huge Queenslander, said, 'Fair go, Boss, she'll be right.'

'It better be.'

With that we were off.

We flew past the Palais de Chaillot, down past the Trocadero fountains, with no time to look in awe at the Eiffel Tower, magnificent and iconic against a purple sky. Further and faster we went, scribbling furiously as DDH gave staccato instructions and observations.

'Champ de Mars, École Militaire, Église du Dome, Rodin museum; see if you can make out the "Thinker" statue in the garden, there by the laurel hedge.'

We raced across the Seine and plunged into the traffic circling Place de Concorde. Adding colour to his tour, DDH told of the guillotine and heads rolling into the baskets of les tricoteuses, the knitting women who sat watching the executions.

'Up there is La Madeleine, and Maxim's restaurant, the most expensive in Paris, is on the left. Somewhere you lot will never eat, for sure.' He laughed at his own dismissive humour.

Ever onwards our van sped into the Parisien night. We crossed the courtyard of the Louvre, pausing only to look through the Arc de Carousel, over the Tuilieries gardens to the Arc de Triomphe in the distance. We rattled onto the cobbles of the Ile de la Cité toward Notre Dame, stopping to view the rear of the Cathedral, the designated centre of Paris. We noted the flying buttresses and caught our breath.

'Not tonight, but with a group you can stop here so they can stretch their legs and use the toilets down the steps. A maximum 30-minute stop.'

Heavy contra-flows on Rue de Rivoli slowed our approach via Sebastopol up to Pigalle, Mont Martre and Sacre Coeur. DDH gave us wise words that now, 30 years later, ring particularly true.

'Mont Martre is beautiful, but the way tourism is swamping this city, it will be overrun, and coaches will be banned for sure. It will be funicular or walking only. So, make the most of it in the next year or two.'

The night swept on. We drove via République to Bastille and followed Rivoli to Hotel de Ville where DDH pulled the van to a halt.

Impressive with the ease with which he passed on information, DDH explained, 'I've stopped here because this building has not only witnessed many historic events, but also the architecture demonstrates a number of styles that are relevant throughout Europe. They give you simple clues to the way European history has evolved from ancient to modern. The easiest way to describe the historical context is by looking at the columns.' He held up his hand to point at the building. 'There are three types of columns. First, the one with the flat, square, uncomplicated top is Doric, reflecting the simple, Doric era. Then you have the scholarly scrolls of the learned Ionic period and finally the aesthetic, sporty Corinthians with the leafy, burnished design.' He paused to allow the information to sink in and then slowly, as if speaking to children, said, 'Doric, Ionic and Corinthian. Remember this because it is relevant all over Europe.'

Our Parisian night tour education was coming to an end. We drove past Opera, along Fauborg St Denis where we located La Folies Bergère, then drove back to Avenue Friedland and parked. A silent anticipation engulfed the van.

'Well, gentlemen.' DDH spoke calmly. 'This is it. We are now going to do the night tour a few times. Tobes, you're first.'

I don't know why I was picked. Perhaps he knew it was not my first visit to Paris or that I had A-level History. More probably it was because I was hiding at the back of the van.

However, even though I made mistakes, my drama teaching background provided me the confidence to present adequately and we arrived back at the Étoile an hour later in fairly good shape. It was now past midnight and the anxiety levels in the van were building as we envisaged more hours and a daylight finish.

After a brief comfort break in the bushes on Rue Beaujou, Ladbroke delivered an acceptable night tour with DDH allowing us to assist with directions; 'or we won't get this done at all,' he reasoned. 'By the way, I am driving tonight, but in the next six weeks we will be sharing the wheel duties.'

This news we welcomed, thinking it would give us the opportunity to relax, drive and not have to bother with learning history and note-taking. We should be so lucky! He explained that we would, of course, have to catch up on notes in our spare time. We also were quickly to learn that driving in Barcelona, Athens, Rome and Istanbul, to name but a few cities, would be anything but relaxing. In the days to come, city tour driving would be considered the short straw when daily tasks were dispensed.

'Right, Marys, that's two tours done well enough. Here is the deal. If the next tour is completed okay we'll call it a night.' We cheered. Desperate for sleep, even in a cold tent, we had seen enough of Paris from within a cramped van.

'Scraps, you're up next.'

Scraps, or Mark Lacy by real name, was a "Freshie". A North Shore Sydney boy, he is to this day happiest with a surfboard under his feet and a cricket bat or rugby ball in his hand. Describing European history and demonstrating cultural understanding with microphone in hand were certainly foreign activities to him.

Gripping the small hand mike, he started.

'Good evening, guys. We are going to head off over the Étoile, which is a twelve-star roundabout that commemorates the war that was started by Baron Haussman.'

We all burst out laughing at the amazing interpretation and misunderstanding of the unique, but unconnected, elements of Parisian context. The van slammed to a halt again.

'Laugh. You should be crying. You better help Lacy out or we're out all night. One out of 45 days to go!'

Scraps was panicking, his easy Aussie drawl now replaced with squeaky, anxious tones. Not wishing to let his mates down, he concentrated hard on giving directions, providing a commentary and reading his notes in the dark. Pulling his moustache with unconscious, nervous energy he ploughed on. We willed him on, prompting, correcting directions and miraculously we passed The Eiffel Tower, Rodin, The Louvre and Concorde. It was three-thirty am when we finally stopped outside the Hotel de Ville.

The building façade was glowing gold from uplights. Their brightness blacked out the surrounding buildings and street. Peering through the van windows we gazed, for the fourth time that night, at this historic building; the heart of Paris. Together with the Louvre nearby, this was the place where kings, emperors, revolutionaries, German conquerors, Allied liberators and rioting students had battled in the creation of French history.

The night somehow became still. This could be the moment we could finish and go to sleep. DDH sat silent in the driver's seat. You could have cut the air of expectancy with a knife. We were all silently mouthing the spiel as Scraps began.

'At this moment we are looking at the Hotel de Ville, the central building in Paris. The Mayor lives here and we can imagine the history of revolution, Louis XIV and the Germans and Allies all milling around.' It was not elegant but demonstrated a grasp of the topic that Scraps could work on. We were nearly there.

'You can also see the columns that hold up the front of the building.' Clearly Scraps was no structural engineer, but he was in the groove. He licked his drying lips. 'You should take the chance to spot some architectural things that we'll see all over Europe.'

It wasn't Clarke's "Civilisation" admittedly, but Scraps was getting there. We were like nodding toy dogs, eyes fixed on him, silently urging from his lips the sweet words that would take us back to our sleeping bags.

Scraps launched into his coup de grace.

'You see those columns, the one with the flat top, the one with the sort of scrolls and the one with a lot of leaves pointing upwards? They are Doric, Ionic and Bionic...'

'Aaahhh! Corinthian!' Ten voices yelled together, the sheer force knocking Scraps backwards from the Tour Guide's perch on the central front engine cover. Our abuse quickly died to silence as we looked for DDH's reaction. Could we be in for another five hours of night tour? Would Scraps be dumped at the railway station? We averted our eyes as DDH turned his head. He was speechless. But not in anger; tears of laughter ran down his face. It was infectious. Guffaws and belly churning laughter burst from us and enveloped the van for at least five minutes. The tensions and anxieties of the first day poured from us. Attempts to speak made it worse. The only person not belly-laughing was Scraps.

'What's so funny?' he kept asking. But eventually he corpsed too and thirty minutes later, around four in the morning, we pulled into the campsite.

'Right, Marys, we will do it all again tomorrow morning, then drive to Lyon. Muff, you'll be first on the mike. Spoof and Wanker, you prepare breakfast for 8am. Goodnight.'

Exhausted, we climbed fully clothed into freezing sleeping bags. In one day our lives had changed.

The following 44 days were, as I am sure you can imagine, full of incident; not to mention earthquakes. We travelled via Barcelona, Nice, Pisa, Florence, Rome, Naples, Sorrento, Capri, Brindisi, Corfu, Athens, Mykonos, Kavalla, Istanbul, Sofia, Skopje, and Dubrovnik, where after a very long walk and a lift on a tractor-trailer, we spent two days relaxing and writing up notes before the replacement van arrived. Then we sped on on to Zadar, Venice, Vienna, Salzburg, Hopfgarten, Munich, Lauterbrunnen, Heidelberg, Amsterdam and all points in between. Finally, saying goodbye, because we would no longer be travelling together, our group returned to London and we began our careers as Tour Guides.

For my part, on return to London, I had two days, in DDH's words to: 'Get your shit together, have a shave and a haircut, buy some clothes that don't make you look like a stupid hippy. You take the first three-weeker leaving on Monday. Good luck, you've got potential. Don't fuck up.'

Such words of positive encouragement from our intrepid leader were rare. And so my life on the road had begun.

3

Russia

The border guard looked up from my passport and stared directly at me. 'Welcome to Russia, Mr Tobin.'

I thought immediately of the Nazi officer in the film, *Where Eagles Dare*. He was tall, blond, upright. He even had a scar on his cheek. Judging by his air of authority my inquisitor was one of the senior staff.

In accented, but excellent, English he asked, 'Are you a regular visitor to Russia?'

'I have been once or twice,' my dry mouth replied without thinking.

He fixed me with a stare. 'This is your fourth visit this year, Mr Tobin. Bring your bag and follow me. My colleagues will see to the rest of your group.'

Taking a deep breath against a rush of anxiety and internally cursing my glib mouth, I followed him across the large, hangar–like room with grey metal tables and chairs, concrete floor and faded paintwork. One or two from my group were stood in front of a table, suitcases open, their belongings laid out in a row. A guard was systematically working his way through the contents.

My man led me into a small ante-room with a curtained cubicle.

'Take your clothes off and put your suitcase on the table if you please. Leave your underpants on.'

Cutting an elegant figure in Marks & Spencer's finest, I watched as an assistant went through my stuff. The Boss concentrated on my handbag or "poofter-bag" as we called it. Used for carrying the all-important documents, cash and travelers cheques, it was my most treasured possession.

He looked closely at my Russian visa which was a separate photocard stapled to a page in my passport. Then he expertly counted the traveler's cheques and foreign cash and matched them against the currency declaration form that I had completed on arrival at the border.

'Do you have any more foreign currency in cash?'

He held up the Swedish and Norwegian Krona, US Dollars and Deutschmarks in the bag.

'No that's all of it.' I swallowed and licked my drying lips.

'Do you have any hashish?'

'No.'

'Do you have any hashish or money on the bus?' The questions came quickly.

'No.'

'Do you know we are searching the bus now?'

'Yes.'

'Will we find anything?'

'Yes. I mean no. Of course not,' I added with a nervous smile.

'How many in your group including you and the driver?'

'Forty three.'

'I know.' He nodded. 'Where are you going?'

'Leningrad, Kalinin, Moscow, Smolensk, Minsk then Poland.'

'I know.' He held my eyes for a long second, then said, 'Thank you. Your passport and those of your group will be returned when we have finished. Get dressed and wait outside.'

It always took at least two hours to cross the border into Russia. Although they clearly enjoyed a rummage through western stuff, in my experience the Russian border guards were always correct. Not friendly, and not unfriendly but strict and methodical. However, this was the first time I had been individually questioned by someone more senior and I was surprised by his specific knowledge.

I blinked in the sunshine outside the main building. One or two trucks, a couple of buses and a few cars were parked in a line as they waited their turn to be inspected. The rest of the massive frontier parking area of Vyborg was empty. In 1980 no one entered — or left — Russia save a few adventurous tourists and officials, and some local Finns who had permission to ply their business across the border. It was still Cold War time. The US had boycotted the Olympics earlier that year and the atmosphere remained military, suspicious and very different.

I looked across to the vast vehicle inspection area where our lone yellow Mercedes coach was parked. Guards were crawling over and under it. Everything packed in the lockers had been emptied onto the concrete floor. The cooking unit had been dismantled and all the tents, including the large cook tent, had been unrolled neatly on the floor. A guard with a sniffer dog worked his way steadily over the equipment.

To keep out of the way, I walked 70 metres over to a clump of trees in front of which was a pile of cardboard egg trays. A large pot was boiling on a camping stove with a gas bottle attached. Margie, our supercook, shrugged her shoulders at me as she watched the pot boil. An armed guard stood nearby eating an egg sandwich.

'They won't let me take fresh eggs across the border, so I persuaded Ivan here,' she gave him a thumbs up, 'to let me cook them. We can have eggs for lunch, dinner and tomorrow's breakfast!'

Boiling ten dozen eggs at the Russian border was not the ordinary thing to do, but there was nothing ordinary about Margie O'Shea. Standing five feet two inches in her best shoes, Margie was one special lady. Best described as an Aussie who should have been Irish, her impersonation skills ranged from Groucho Marx to Humphrey Bogart and her gift of the gab could reduce the most belligerent of characters to tears of laughter.

Margie was a brilliant companion to have on our road crew team; she was our cook and Rabbit, our driver. I was Tour Leader. It was our task to lead our 40 customers on a four-week trip around Scandinavia and Russia. Our group consisted of Aussies and Kiwis, about two-thirds were female and all were between the age of 18 to 35. We were travelling in a "Big Yellow" coach with a large smiley sun painted on the side. In 1980 pre–perestroika, pre-glasnost Russia we certainly turned a few heads.

Several hours later, driving east, away from the border at Vyborg, the afternoon sunlight shone across the flat waters of the Gulf of Finland. Pine trees and dunes lined the seascape. Fishermen tugged handlines from flat-bottomed skiffs anchored a few hundred metres off shore. Like an impressionist painting, the natural beauty was a stark contrast to the shabby wooden or pre-fabricated concrete houses and drab clothing of the locals. The potholed road was busy with filthy, exhaust-spewing trucks, listing and gurgling their way on the main route to Leningrad.

Making headway in eighties Russia was slow. Rabbit drove as fast as the potholes would allow, veering and winding from one side of the road to the other, playing a dangerous game of dodgems with oncoming vehicles doing the same. There was no established traffic code and the sudden appearance of horses, carts and even pedestrians in the middle of the road added to the challenge. It came as no surprise to learn that year of a tragic accident, when an old truck careered into a broken-down tour bus parked at the roadside. The driver, an acquaintance of ours, was sadly killed as he worked on the engine.

The road followed the coastline for kilometre after kilometre. To our right were dunes, deserted beaches and shining sea; to our left, inland, dense pine forests interspersed with the occasional grey, dreary village.

About 20 kilometers from Leningrad, a car overtook us and flashed its lights on and off a few times.

'Here's Yevgeny,' said Rabbit and we followed the car as it turned off into a wide parking area that offered dramatic views over the Gulf. We let our troops off the coach to smoke, stretch their legs, admire the view and relieve themselves amongst the gorse bushes.

'Girls to the left, boys to the right on bush stops,' was the common instruction at the start of each tour when explaining the *modus operandi* for impromptu comfort breaks. On trips such as these, we had long distances to cover and no onboard toilet. Facilities in Russia, Eastern Europe and North Africa were either non-existent or beyond dreadful. Within a couple of days everyone became used to the routine. 'No-one gives a hoot when it comes to ablute,' was how Margie described it.

Yevgeny waved hello and I walked over to the car.

'Tobarovitch, you bastard!' He gave me a hug that lifted me off my feet. 'It is great to see you. How was the border?'

'A little slow. They were interested in foreign currency. Probably after those issues at the Olympic campsite.'

Yevgeny laughed. 'They have no imagination! So, my friend what have you got?'

'A hundred 501's and the Gibson guitar you wanted.'

'Really? That's fantastic. It got through OK?'

'We just left it on the luggage rack with Rab's guitar. Apparently they opened the case, checked with the dog and that was that.'

Yevgeny grinned and lit the Marlborough cigarette Rabbit offered him. He savoured the hit of western tobacco and blew a long stream of smoke in the air. Yevgeny was our fixer. Operating outside the official government tourism system, Intourist, he ran a black-market business buying Levi jeans and other western goods from the few tourist groups that visited Russia in the late seventies and eighties.

The system was simple but carried an element of risk. Before entering Russia, I would buy fifty or so pairs of Levi jeans and distribute one, or maximum two, pairs to each person in the group. At the border the odd pair of jeans in each suitcase did not raise suspicion, once the labels had been removed. At our first night stop the driver and I would discreetly collect up the jeans and hide them on the coach, ready to meet up with Yevgeny and do the trade the following day in such a way that the Intourist guide, who would be with us for the trip, suspected nothing. Yevgeny would pay us a generous cash price in roubles and we would fund our entire trip and our customers' spending money throughout Russia, living like kings in our attempt to spend all the roubles, which were worthless outside of Russia.

The customers loved the secrecy and minor subterfuge and were happy to repay us for the loan in Deutschmarks later in the trip. We gave them an excellent exchange rate, which was also very profitable for the crew. The same principle applied to company expenses. Once we had developed a friendship with Yevgeny over a few visits we took on more challenging imports, such as the Gibson Les Paul guitar on this trip.

'So, when will your group go to Petrodvorets?'

Yevgeny was referring to the included riverboat excursion from the centre of Leningrad out to the stunning eighteenth century summer gardens of the Tsars. Whilst the group, accompanied by our Intourist guide, took the three-hour trip, the driver and I would exchange goods with Eugene, sort the roubles, fuel the coach and celebrate with vodka and caviar from the Caspian Sea.

'We meet our guide tomorrow morning at the campsite. Assume we will do a city tour as usual and be at the boat wharf by Alexander Bridge at 2pm.'

'Time to go,' said Rab. The troops were back on the coach.

The light was fading as we pulled away leaving Yevgeny waving from the nondescript Lada car, his ever-present, silent companion, Leo, behind the wheel.

The next day, I woke to a bright morning, grabbed my wash-bag, towel and date roll (an Aussie term for toilet paper) and walked the hundred metres from my tent across dried mud and wood chippings to the shower block of the official Intourist Leningrad Campsite.

Like all state-run campsites, and most institutions, everything was run down. The public rooms were flaking and musty, shower units were basic with cold water and the toilets unspeakably grim. Maintenance or basic upkeep was minimal. No-one gave a damn; State or workers.

Margie had breakfast underway in the cook tent, a portable marquee we erected at each night stop. Tea, coffee, cold boiled eggs, black bread and vegemite were on the menu. Suitably refreshed, and in a clean T-shirt I walked over to the office to meet our Intourist guide.

Every group visiting Russia had to be accompanied by an official guide. They were well-educated, young state workers who had been chosen for their language skills and for their rare commitment to doing a good job. They were invaluable to us in dealing with Russian bureaucracy and the endless form-filling required to visit the palaces, monasteries, museums and galleries of Leningrad and Moscow.

Often the same age as us, the guides generated genuine interest amongst our groups and on the long bus journeys we would debate the pros and cons of the Cold War and the cultural differences of East and West. The contrast between our self-indulgent, libertarian, freedom-assuming western lifestyle and the state-governed, restricted, introspective world of Russia was stark.

Despite their clear envy of our freedom to travel and live as we chose, and despite living a life of relative hardship from our western point of view, every guide demonstrated an absolute pride and love for their "Mother" Russia, which we found impressive and worthy of respect.

Our guide for this trip, Marsha, was waiting in the office. She was petite with long blonde hair framing her strikingly attractive face and large pointed nose. I was smitten immediately when, blushing slightly, Marsha said, 'Good morning,' in an accent so beautifully foreign that the words sounded like "Je t'aime" breathed by Jane Birkin to Serge Gainsbourg.

We agreed on the plans for the day, which meant the meeting with Yevgeny would be as arranged, and we all piled onto the coach and headed the ten kilometers into the centre of Leningrad.

Formerly St Petersburg, and today renamed St Petersburg, Leningrad was and is a wonderful city; the Venice of the North, City of Tsars, founded on the banks of the river Neva by Peter the Great. The central part of the city consists almost entirely of classical eighteenth century architecture. The Hermitage is the world-renowned art gallery that rivals the Louvre; then there are the Peter and Paul Cathedral and fortress, the Admiralty and the baroque Winter Palace, so spectacular in turquoise and gold. There are three Cathedrals, the summer gardens of the Tsars, Battleship Potemkin and, for the more "cultural" among us, a couple of the most atmospheric vodka drinking halls you will ever see. Champagne, vodka and brandy by the case, with potato, beetroot and cucumber nibbles for the masses, and caviar and herring for VIPs.

I introduced Marsha to our group and they seemed as enchanted as I was by her shy delivery when she took a moment to introduce herself. She described her work as a guide with Intourist, and what life was like at college in Moscow and in the small apartment she shared with her parents. She relished the opportunity to travel with people from Australia and New Zealand and loved listening to the Beatles and the Carpenters and drinking Pepsi Cola. Marsha's charm was so compelling that the whole group was spellbound and eager to interact. She told us that although she lived in Moscow, her favourite city was Leningrad and she wanted us to see as much of it as possible.

Marsha was right. The city tour of Leningrad is awe-inspiring. We needed first to negotiate the potholed ring road through

23

the outer city of tenement blocks and faceless State buildings, but when we crossed our first bridge over a tributary of the Neva we were swept into the eighteenth century world of the Tsars. Grandeur and classical architecture abounded — with many examples of Doric, Ionic and Corinthian styles! We caught a glimpse of the Peter and Paul Cathedral as we crossed the Alexander III bridge of which there is a copy in Paris. We turned onto the impossibly wide Nevsky Prospect and followed the tram tracks down this grand avenue towards St Isaac's cathedral. A couple of black official limousines sped past in the reserved central lanes; a perfect example of the privileges retained for the elite few.

As we turned in to the Palace square the first sight of the Winter Palace, painted in rich greens and trimmed like a Christmas cake in gold leaf, drew "wows" from Marsha's audience. We finally halted outside the Hermitage Museum, which occupied a whole side of the massive square.

Marsha was a real hit with our group. She made fun of the "washerwomen" who work the Hermitage reception area as ticket attendants. Their lazy jobsworth attitude could make entry to one of the world's truly great museums unbearable. However, Marsha was used to their ways and simply handed them a list of names and ushered the group through. Her diminutive form belied the authoritative manner with which she dismissed the meaningless bureaucracy.

The Hermitage has four hundred rooms and over three million works of art. It was also the headquarters of Kerensky's provisional government set up after the death of Nicholas II. Although overthrown by the Bolsheviks in 1917 the art collection was preserved. Our group of forty young antipodeans padding along the ancient, wooden corridors, like lost surf bums, must have looked as anachronistic as three hundred Spartans marching up Peckham High Street.

A two-hour visit does not even begin to scratch the surface of the Hermitage, but it was enough for us and soon it was time to head down to the Hotel Astoria for coffee and a visit to their plush washrooms. I do like to think that by osmosis some of the creative wonder and world-shaping history might have been taken in by members of our group and they would be enriched by the experience, but at the end of the day, if asked for the highlight of the city tour, most would vote for the Astoria's dunnys.

However fascinating the city tour was, and however mesmerizing Marsha, the clock was ticking towards the meeting with Yevgeny. Although I had made the trade a few times before, there was still enough risk in it to keep my mind focused and gnaw at my stomach. Spot on two o'clock, as we waved Marsha and the troops off on their three-hour trip to Petrodvorets, the maroon Lada pulled up in front of the coach. Yevgeny waved from the passenger seat and beckoned us to follow. We drove away from the riverside boulevard and down a quieter street where tall buildings and trees cut out the sun. The darkened light only added to Rabbit's and my sense of tension. At the end of the street we turned into a small, tree-lined square with a large revolutionary statue in the centre.

The Lada stopped under a tree and Yevgeny was out and in a flash onto our coach.

'We do it here. It's safe,' he said with a reassuring grin and a wind-emptying slap on my back.

Rab opened the locker underneath the coach and we grabbed the large black sacks full of jeans and chucked them onto the back seat of the Lada. I slid the guitar, in its case, from the luggage rack and handed it to Yevgeny who put it in the car.

Leo, nodding a speechless greeting, opened the boot of the car. His huge hands, on the end of heavily muscled, tattooed arms easily lifted the carpet floor.

Rab whistled softly. In place of the spare tyre there were blocks and blocks of cash held in rubber bands or wrapped in newspaper. We could also make out the snub nose of a pistol and what looked like a small machine gun. Yevgeny counted out blocks of cash and put them in a brown paper bag. He also took from his pocket a great wad of notes wrapped with elastic.

'There are Roublis for the 501s and Swedish Kroner for the guitar. I give you hard currency as you never spend enough roubli. Come, take me on your bus and I will be your Intourist guide for an hour!' he laughed.

Leo wordlessly closed the boot and drove off with a brief nod of "dosvedanya".

We stashed the money in the floor well of the coach and Yevgeny directed us a kilometer or so to an imposing, column-façaded mansion. With the coach parked outside, we pushed open the double doors to reveal a vast dining hall with high arched ceilings. Tall, sashed windows pulled searchlight beams of sunshine into the wood paneled room. There were refectory tables with groups of men eating and drinking noisily. No-one paid us any attention, although Rab and I stood out somewhat, wearing T-shirts, jeans and Dutch clogs. We drank a straw-coloured champagne accompanied by shots of vodka. An old waiter served dishes of potato salad with beetroot and herring and grinned toothlessly at us.

Yevgeny ignored all my questions about his operation with a smile and upended a half full bottle of vodka into a large silver tureen of ice cream.

'Enjoy, my friends. Enjoy mother Russia!'

Later, sucking in air to sober up, Rabbit and I stood by the coach as our troops, accompanied by Marsha, got off the hydrofoil and boarded the coach.

'Did you have a nice lunch?' Marsha innocently asked. 'Where did you go?'

'Oh, just the Astoria as usual.'

'Of course.' Her smiling eyes easily pierced my lying heart.

That evening was a "national meal" event. Marsha had booked a spacious Georgian restaurant that was well regarded for its delicacies and good wine. Much to everyone's delight, champagne, vodka and brandy were also included in the price. A pop band dressed in sparkling suits with a fabulously energetic female singer played Abba and Beatles songs. Our group, made up of mostly gorgeous Aussie blondes, with their best frocks on and fuelled to the hilt on champagne and brandy, was a real hit with the VIP locals and Finnish businessmen.

I spent most of the evening like a tail-wagging spaniel at the side of little Marsha. She laughed and clapped at my jokes and chatted engagingly about literature and art, but she refused to dance and would not let me kiss her on the cheek or hold her hand.

She bent close. 'I cannot, Simon. People know me here. I like you, so you can call me Marshenka; when no-one else can hear.'

Her hand brushed my wrist. I had to battle not to explode on the spot.

The end of the evening arrived, and it was time to round up our troops and herd them on to the coach. It took a while as we good-naturedly extracted them from trysts and final passionate embraces. Apart from the usual alcohol wobbles, there were no issues or missing persons and we got everyone outside. In the chill cold, however, the atmosphere changed. As we crossed the road unsteadily to the waiting coach, two of our last tottering ladies were grabbed by three big guys. Despite the screaming the men began to drag them back towards the restaurant.

Before I could react, two figures appeared from behind our coach, crossed the road in a flash and in a flurry of arms and kicks, poleaxed the three men in seconds. Mildly, they then escorted the stunned girls on to the coach.

Leo nodded to me and walked away. Yevgeny wiped his hand on his new Levis.

'Be safe, Tobovaritch. See you next time.' And he was gone.

'A friend?' Marsha breathed in my ear from the seat behind me as we drove away.

Moscow came and went. Despite dreary weather, Marsha's stories brought the city alive. The troops were amazed by the size of Red Square and the Kremlin. The bright colours of St Basil's Cathedral drew more "wows". To Marsha's and local bystander's astonishment we performed "dead ants" in the Gum department store.

'You can be so childish,' scolded Marsha as we walked back from Lenin's Tomb to the coach pick up point. Then she flashed me a smile and it stopped raining.

Our Russian chapter closed as we headed west from Moscow via Minsk to the border with Poland and the road to Warsaw, then Berlin. It was a long journey to the border which involved an overnight stop in Smolensk.

Around midday we pulled off the road onto an open parking ground surrounded by gorse and woodland. While most took a "bush stop", Rab, Margie, Marsha and I wandered over to a roadside stall selling enormous watermelons.

'They come from this area,' explained Marsha, 'and they are

28

known for the sweetness.'

We bought a half dozen with a few roubles and two Marlborough cigarettes. The stallholder, already on his second western fag, wheeled the melons to the coach on a makeshift wheelbarrow, taking the opportunity to eye the Aussie and Kiwi girls in shorts and bikini tops playing French cricket and eating black bread vegemite sandwiches. With a large kitchen knife Rabbit sawed the top off each pale green melon. We cut and spooned the pink fruit inside into a large pot. Margie handed out spoons to everyone and soon all 44 of us, including Marsha were slurping the juiciest melon pieces we had ever tasted. Into each melon shell we emptied three bottles of vodka and Rab fixed each top back on with gaffer tape. We wedged the six alcohol bombs into the luggage compartment and continued to Smolensk.

'If God was going to give the world an enema, Smolensk campsite is where he'd put the tube.' This was what "Hanoi" had announced a few years ago, on a training tour of Russia and Scandinavia. Only capable Tour Leaders were trained in Russia because of the subterfuge needed, and the requirement to be able to think on your feet. The London office or friendly local suppliers were not easily on hand to help if required. You had to sort things out yourself. Hanoi's real name was Paul, but his nickname referred to his ability to get bombed every night.

'You have no choice but to stop in Smolensk,' he told us. 'Intourist specify where and when you stop. No skipping stuff by doing overnight drives. Because you have to be here, you need to arrange a party to take people's minds off this dump!' Hanoi's ability to party was legendary, so every Tour Leader decided to follow suit. Smolensk meant party!

When we arrived, the few site workers who were used to a "Big Yellow" passing through every two weeks were already waiting to help us put the tents up and chain smoke as many Marlboroughs as they could get their hands on. After a few shots of vodka and some warm Russian beer we were pitched. A camp fire was lit, and our tents circled the central cook tent, a circle of colour amid a vast area of grey, dried mud flecked with grass. It looked as if we were awaiting an Apache raid.

The site was surrounded with chain fencing and backed on to a dense forest, so the setting had a compound feel that gave rise to jokes about *The Great Escape*. A few even went as far as doing PT exercises and pretending to put soil down their trouser legs. Rab and I took on more vodka and, accompanied by two site workers who were bribed with fags, marched over to the disgusting toilet block with buckets and brushes. We managed to get one loo just about bearable. There were no showers in Smolensk.

Dinner was a delicious tinned tuna with pasta. I was always amazed by how Margie, and all the cooks I worked with, could create such terrific food in sometimes the most trying of circumstances. We washed down supper with cocktails served straight from the big melon gourds. We had no ice, but the blisteringly potent warmish melon slush slipped down a treat. Marsha arrived with a worker carrying a box full of tiny cartons of excellent vanilla ice cream for dessert.

It had been a meal fit for royalty and, to celebrate, Rab's guitar came out. Around the campfire we sang our way through his repertoire of Jim Croce and Beach Boys songs. The melon demolished, we turned to warm champagne and brandy. Under the sparkling stars of the Byelorussian night the Kiwis sang Maori songs. Then Marsha stood up and called the site staff who had been hovering in the background. We gave them drinks and they sang so passionately that we all had to join in, clapping, singing and dancing; trying to reach the strangely deep tones of the Russian boatmen of the Volga we had heard in films. Cossack dancing is not best attempted on a belly full of melon vodka, champagne and brandy.

As the fire reduced to glowing embers and the night drew in, there were bodies everywhere. Some slept with feet hanging out of tents, some sprawled where they lay on sleeping lilos they had pulled around the fire. Others merely collapsed against each other in alcoholic oblivion. Russia's spell had bewitched us.

I awoke with a jolt in the dark. Where was I? My mouth was dry and foul, my body ached as I lay on the plastic ground sheet on the floor. There was a weight on my chest. My brain was still disconnected from my body as I felt her silky hair and sensed her breathing. Gently I eased myself alongside her tiny frame and wrapped my arm around her. She murmured sleepy pleasure and stirred backwards into my body shape, seeking closeness. She purred as I slipped my hand under her T-shirt and slowly stroked upward. Marsha gasped and shot upright.

'What are we doing, Simon. Where are we?'

'It's OK. It's OK... It's OK,' I implored, my hand still under her T-shirt, her nipple swollen against my fingertips.

Marsha looked down at me. With a deep sigh she took my hand, held it against her breast for a moment, then gently pushed it away.

'Although I want, I cannot, Simon. They will know and I will lose my job. I must go.'

The coach was very quiet that morning with lots of sunglasses on faces, despite the rain. We stopped at the Intourist office on the outskirts of Minsk to drop off Marsha, before we headed to the Polish border and to new adventures in Warsaw and beyond. The group sang "For she's a jolly good fellow" to Marsha and we gave her our remaining roubles. She was shocked by the amount and gave me a knowing look.

We kissed briefly, and she walked away. On my seat she had left a book of short stories by Turgenev. Inside she had written an inscription.

"Read this and think of me. Your Marshenka."

4

France

Any memoir of mine could not be complete without a chapter on France. This was the country that first gave me the taste for travel and stirred a passion in me that I had not felt before. It had started in the 60s, bouncing down the RN7 in the family Zephyr to the Arcachon basin, south of Bordeaux. I loved sliding down the Pyla sand dune, tasting my first dish of moules frites, smelling the heat of the Medoc. We dived directly from the beach into the deep-sea channel at Cap Ferret and drank citron presse in the small campsite bar.

School trips to Normandy and Paris and learning to ski in Chamonix only added to the magnetism of France for me. It was therefore no surprise that I took my first job abroad as a kayak instructor in the Ardeche Gorge in Southern France. This was a life changing time. Barefoot and wearing the same pair of shorts all summer, I lived on riverbanks under canvas, swimming and teaching canoeing every day in rushing waters. There were evening campfires; my skin was nut brown from the Midi sun and my teeth stained from cheap red wine and acrid Celtas cigarettes.

At the end of that summer there was no chance of me returning to the UK to teach, so I set off for India. However, destitution brought me home within weeks. After a day or two of Mother's cooking I had answered an advert in a free London paper and began life as a Tour Guide.

It was soon after I had finished my first summer season of guiding that I received a phone call.

'Glad I've tracked you down.' It was Hook, the Operations Manager on the phone. The derivation of his nickname shall remain a mystery. DDH was a good mate of his. 'We've bought a Chateau in the Beaujolais, near Lyon and we would like you to spend the winter down there and help to do it up.'

The first summer of Tour Guiding was over and I had been contemplating work in a ski resort, when this unexpected invitation arrived. Taken by the Aussie/Kiwi camaraderie and full of desire to continue working as a Tour Guide the following year, I accepted immediately.

'You leave Waterloo tomorrow at 6am sparrows for Paris,' Hook said. 'Grappa is going with you. Meet him at 0545 under the clock. He will have the tickets. There is a milk train leaves Gare de Lyon in the evening. Be on it and get off at Villefranche-sur-Saone, the stop before Lyon. Dick Parry will meet you. Put the work in and enjoy.'

Clarity of purpose, be positive, no fucking about, get on with it. I enjoyed the Antipodean way of doing things and had learned fast in that first summer, so I wasn't fazed by Hook's lack of conversational telephone manner.

It was early morning when Grappa, whose nickname describes his affection for the Italian firewater, and I, climbed in to the VW van outside Villefranche station.

Dick sniffed disapprovingly. 'I sense you had one or two on

the way down.'

'Bloody oath, and we met a couple of Swedish sorts too.' Grappa was in great form.

'One or two, Dick and thanks for picking us up. We are really looking forward to this.' I tried to sound as sober as I could.

'Fine. Remember, we are here to work first and play later.'

Dick had been given the serious responsibility of managing the project to transform a nineteenth century chateau, in reasonable repair in the Beaujolais countryside, into a fully functioning "Special Stopover" for our European tour groups. They would leave Paris, stay overnight in the Chateau and then continue to either Barcelona or Nice, depending on the itinerary. The Chateau de Cruix would need to accommodate two groups; over 100 guests plus staff.

I stared out of the window at the Beaujolais countryside. Narrow lanes circled steep, green, sometimes rocky, hills covered with vines. It was early January so the grapevines had a shorn, wizened character. I thought of rows of Giacometti sculptures.

The road narrowed further as we chugged past stone cottages with terracotta roofs. Although early in the year, the sun was shining. We were definitely in the South.

Beaujolais is a region relatively untouched by the tourist bootprint. Most travellers stay on the A6 motorway as it sweeps past Villefranche and on to Lyon, the second city of France. The Beaujolais stands silently apart, its small villages hidden among the stony hills and green valleys. Winemaking is the preeminent activity. Each village has a cooperative that produces very passable wine and there are a number of higher quality producers who are world-renowned.

The red grape is Gamay, which produces young, refreshing, fruity wine. Some of the nobler names can age well but for the most part Beaujolais is to be drunk when it is young, and often in considerable quantities. Please ignore the marketing rubbish of Beaujolais Nouveau and drink wines a year or two old at least!

Dick turned the van onto a narrow track leading to a hamlet of terracotta farmhouses and a scattering of barns and wine chais, or above-ground cellars. The engine echoed against the stone walls as we drove past and up to two tall gateposts and iron gates at the end of the track.

We drove through the gates and crunched onto a gravel drive edged with beech trees. The drive opened to reveal rambling, terraced and unkempt grounds dotted with tall cedar trees. The Chateau stood above the grounds on a rise fronted by a long, paved terrace with a waist-high balustrade that ran the whole length. The building itself was impressively grandiose, cornered by square towers and slate turrets. The façade had an Italianate feel with banks of long symmetrical windows, mostly covered with closed shutters. Although the whole place needed some care and attention, the faded elegance had considerable appeal.

'Wow, it's huge.'

'It's fantastic.'

'Sure is,' said Dick, 'and we've got four months to get it ship shape and ready to feed, sleep and entertain two groups every night.'

Dick had a team of seven of us, unskilled but willing company staff, to handle cleaning, painting, gardening, humping and very basic handyman work. Local builders, artisans, electricians and plumbers had been contracted for the serious renovations. Evidence of their work was everywhere with vans, mixers, pipes and bags of plaster laid to the side of the building and a number of men in travail bleus moving about purposefully. However, in the ensuing weeks, we found them not so purposeful as to refuse a smoke and a glass when one was offered.

Dick's French was fair, but he was grateful to have Karen and Sally as his assistants. Both were fluent French speakers, so they spent most of their time cajoling workers, making endless telephone calls and battling the French bureaucracy. All meals were provided by Annie, the chef and kitchen organiser.

On our first full day, bleary after a Beaujolais welcome session, we pick-axed and dug out the entrance driveway and removed a few small trees to allow for coach access. Dick had imposed a daily alcohol ban until 6 pm, to which we reluctantly pledged agreement. So when Annie called us in for lunch of soup and baguette, we drank cordial and tea.

'Good start, boys,' said Dick. 'Tonight, we have been invited to Jean Claude and Simone's for wine tasting and supper.'

That evening, having slurped a couple of early glasses, we crunched down the drive to the large, stone-walled "chais" or wine cellar, on the edge of the hamlet. Jean Claude welcomed us warmly and ushered us in for a taste of his Gamay.

The candlelight flickered on the rough, stone walls and we perched on benches as JC dispensed wine and explained the provenance of Beaujolais wines. Face ruddy from the sun and hands roughened by years in the vineyards, JC was the authentic viticulteur. He loved his drop too, so that by the time Simone came to call us "à table", there were a fair number of empty bottles on the old oak armoir that had served as a tasting table. Grappa announced that the taste of Beaujolais was 'like an angel crying on your tongue,' and swore lifelong allegiance to all French winemakers. 'Particularly this bastard,' he added affectionately, throwing his arm around JC's wide shoulders.

Supper was a delight. Old vines were burning in the open fireplace in the sprawling farmhouse kitchen. The huge table was covered by a red checked tablecloth. We ate plates of charcuterie followed by a daube stew spooned straight from the casserole pot. There was freshly baked bread, a crisp green salad, creamy St Marcellin cheese and finally a tarte aux pruneaux. Our meal was accompanied by litres of Gamay of varying age. Jean Claude insisted we try his vin mousseaux with dessert.

'We do not plant only red,' he explained in English that improved as the night went on. 'I will now demonstrate the sabrassage!'

Simone's eyes rolled in knowing anticipation of catastrophe, as JC held the champagne-style bottle with one hand and, with a large sword that he took from its holder over the fireplace, expertly swept the cork and wire basket off the bottle in one stroke. Some wine gushed, but there was enough remaining to fill our glasses.

'Can I have a go?'

'Me too.'

'And me.'

The seven of us were given a bottle each and armed with kitchen knives, an old wood splitter, the sabre and a battered machete used for poking the fire. We lined up ready to go.

'One, two, three, go!'

Glass and wine flew everywhere. There were one or two successful attempts, but most of us were left holding the bottom of a smashed bottle with its contents running on the stone floor.

JC roared with laughter and Simone removed a cork basket from her blonde hair and smiled. She was completely unperturbed, as if booze and broken glass all over the kitchen was a common occurrence.

'I think you need more practice,' she said.

Later, back at the Chateau, Melbourne Andy took his flute to the great central staircase and the building reverberated with very passable Jethro Tull riffs.

Dick sat at our kitchen table and made the shopping list for the weekly run into Lyon. DIY stuff, food, general supplies and, yes, he would buy a couple of cases of cheap fizz so we could practice our sabrassage skills.

'Karen and Annie will come with me. You can come next time,' he said. 'Tomorrow you can start rubbing down the shutters in preparation for painting'. We felt like kids. Do our homework and we get the treat of a trip to Lyon.

Over breakfast of vegemite toast, all a touch worse for wear, Dick mused,

'What colour should we paint the shutters?'

'British racing green,' I said automatically, as if no other colour should be considered. 'It's classic, won't show the dust and besides, the Wallabies wear a bit of green.'

'And the cricketers wear the baggy,' Grappa added in support.

Dick duly returned with dark green paint and over the following week, from morning to night, we scraped, sanded, primed and painted the lower shutters.

'They look splendid,' said Grappa, his hair the colour of spinach.

It was a sunny morning and the whole team was out on the terrace admiring our work. Through the gates and up the drive came a dented Renault 5. The driver squeezed his large frame out of the car and walked purposefully over to us. He was the Mayor.

'Messieursdames, bonjour. I see you have plentiful painted.' He waved an arm at the shutters. 'Mais vous avez un problem.'

'What's the problem?' asked Karen, in French.

The Mayor spoke again. We caught some of it, but Karen

translated. It seemed that the colour of the shutters wasn't allowed in the Beaujolais region.

'Fuck,' said Spinach head.

The Mayor was extremely cordial, and he accepted a glass of morning Beaujolais and a slice of vegemite toast, which he politely left to one side after the first nibble. Over a second glass, and in ever-improving English, he expressed the village's delight in our project and they looked forward to welcoming Australian visitors, anything he could do, just ask.

'But monsieur must change his hair and paint the shutters in a regional colour of grey or maroon. Au revoir et bon courage!'

'Well, that's a lesson learned,' said Dick.

'He can come again,' said Grappa. 'At least we get a drink before six.'

* * *

'Do you think this place is haunted?' Grappa asked one day from his ladder.

'You never know; that chapel attached to the rear tower could be a home for a vampire, or maybe a virgin was slaughtered there by the local squire.' Melbourne Andy had a vivid imagination. We reckoned it was from too much flute playing.

'No seriously, I hear something every night, like a shuffling of feet. There is a sort of eerie light, too.'

'Nah, it's all bollocks. Probably a cat or a rat.'

'Or a monkey sit upon your knee, an old pol parrot with a beak like a carrot, a large black beetle and a flea.' I sang the old nursery rhyme.

'Fuck you, if you're not going to take it seriously.' Grappa was clearly troubled.

Andy and I hatched a plan while Grappa cleaned the paint brushes. That evening we would ensure he took on plenty of wine, which wouldn't be a problem, and after he retired to bed the Ghost of the Chateau would pay him a visit.

'What's so funny?' he asked after dinner. 'You idiots have been tittering all bloody night.'

'Just remembering the sabrassage.' Everyone, except Grappa, was in on the plan and the supper table had been like a scene at a silent auction, with nods, winks and restrained giggles.

Finally, when Grappa seemed suitably fuelled, and started telling stories he had told earlier, Dick called the proceedings to a halt. 'Let's crash. Big day tomorrow; John Trumpington is coming.'

'G'night.'

'Sweet dreams.'

'Good night, John Boy.'

'Good night, Mary Ellen.'

The Waltons played an important part in our nocturnal ritual.

As arranged, we were all back down in the kitchen half an hour later, except Grappa. The girls had cut two holes in a large white bed sheet, which they threw over my head and secured around my waist with a loose rope. I held a torch under the linen and shone it below my face.

'Turn the lights off. Let's have a look.'

'Wow that is really freaky when you shine that light on your face,' said Sal. 'I'm scared and I know it's you.'

Melbourne Andy blew softly across the mouthpiece of his flute, making a low whistling sound. 'Right, now's the time.'

The six of us climbed the wide stone stairs, shushing each other as we went. We could hear Grappa's snoring from the west wing. The moonlight shone pale grey through the windows. Our shadows danced behind us. We stepped from the stairs on to the wooden corridor and the boards creaked underfoot.

'I'm shitting myself,' whispered Sal elegantly.

'Shh shh shhh!'

We reached Grappa's room. The snoring was raucous. Andy began to blow softly on the flute; I pushed the door open and turned the torch to my face under the sheet.

Sal screamed! I turned and crashed in to Andy.

'What's up?'

'Down there I saw a figure.'

'Quick! It could be a real ghost.'

Like an episode from The Goon Show, we hurtled noisily back along the corridor.

'It was here,' screeched Sal, from behind Dick's back. We flicked the main lights on and Andy ran down the stone stairs, his clogs clanging on the flagstones.

'There's nothing here. Must have been the moonlight.'

We gathered back in the kitchen, with all the lights on.

'I am sure I saw something.'

'Well whatever it was, it's gone.'

'What about Grappa?'

I ran loudly back upstairs, still wearing the ghostly sheet. The door was open, and Grappa lay just as we had left him, snoring like a bull elephant, completely oblivious to the pandemonium.

'He's sparko.' I returned to the kitchen where Dick was serving Beaujolais to calm the nerves. No-one wanted to sleep alone that night, so we dragged our mattresses and sleeping bags down from our bedrooms to the main drawing room and lay there listening intently as the silver moonlight played tricks with our imagination.

'Good night, John Boy.'

'Good night, Mary Ellen.'

It was the earliest breakfast we had eaten. The trials of the previous night had made us ravenous and we were wolfing scrambled eggs and slurping coffee when Grappa emerged.

'God, I slept like a log. What's up with you lot? You look like you've seen a ghost.'

A few hours later our company lawyer arrived from Lyon. He was here to review progress and help with any thorny bits of French bureaucracy. Of a certain age, John Trumpington was an English Francophile who had settled in France years ago. A gourmand, he wore on his faded club tie the record of many gastronomic adventures. JT, as we called him, had been something official in Rome after the successful allied invasion of Italy toward the end of the war.

'They were good times given the circumstances,' he explained with glass in hand. 'The Holy Father managed to keep up his passion for Tuscan food as the world around him was tearing itself apart. He and I would occasionally manage a glass or two of Torgiano with a pasta supper. I also enjoyed putting competitions in the Cardinal's lounge with Patten's major d'omo, although he was dreadfully uncouth; chewed gum and drank Coca Cola with his carbonara, for heaven's sake.'

Whether they were true or not, we loved his anecdotes and his Englishness. There was always a panama hat and a cricket bat on the back seat of his Citroen. Despite appearances he was sharp as a tack and helped enormously, with sage legal advice and tips on French culture.

'Take it as gospel my friends, you will never be fully integrated into the community, but with good manners, a positive approach, a bit of French and a love of food you can make friends and influence people here. Is there a spot of lunch?'

Annie served a creamed spinach starter followed by roast lamb and all the trimmings and a Pavlova for pud.

'Delightful,' JT declared, dabbing his food-speckled tie and draining his glass.

'You chaps do very well here and clearly enjoy a good meal. You should try Bocuse; he's making a real name for himself just along the river south of Lyon. He's created a new form of eating, called Nouvelle Cuisine, making waves everywhere.'

The story of mine and Grappa's subsequent visit to Paul Bocuse, the waiter's icy stare when we asked for salt and pepper and having to call JT to help with the unexpectedly astronomic bill will await another day. For when it comes to stories about lunching there is only one place. Florence.

5

Firenze

E veryone has a favourite Italian city. The uniqueness of Venice mostly wins out over Rome's classics, Naples' frenzy, Milan's cool, Torino's autoculture, Verona's music or Bologna's kitchens. For the Tour Guide, the favourite is most definitely Florence.

It's not for reasons of architectural wonder, though few cities can boast such a view as from Piazzale Michelangelo with Il Duomo standing out above the ochre rooftops like a great puff ball mushroom bursting from the forest floor. Nor is it for reasons of artistic interest, though it is hard to match the renaissance brilliance of the Uffizi and Accademia. Nor even for reasons of style, though the dedicated fashion follower cannot fail but to be tempted by the boutiques between Piazzas Republica and Signora. No. Our affection for Firenze is inspired by the indelible mark three Florentine gentlemen have made on our lives.

Our three musketeers are Paolo Fortini, Walter Gelli and Franco Calamini. They have helped and advised Tour Guides from all parts of the world, introducing civilized behavior to the most "ocker" of Aussies and showing Kiwis how to wind their watches forward from the sleepy corner of the map into the time zone of a modern European lifestyle. As fixers, local suppliers and guides, red tape cutters, arrangers, advisors and unofficial ambassadors of their beloved Firenze, they have been invaluable to all who cross the Arno river into Vecchia Firenze. However, beyond all that, it is the way they live their lives, their *modus vivendi*, that has left the most lasting impression.

Our three Florentines rejoice in daily living, reacting to any moment or issue with laughter and wild gesticulation. Ideas, schemes, fantasies, jokes, passions, stories, family, friends and fiestas fill even the briefest conversations. Add to this joie de vivre the delights of vine and table, and their spontaneous passion for living reaches epic proportions. It is in the simple phrase "Let's go for lunch" that a world of endless possibility is revealed to those who meet Signori Fortini, Gelli and Calamini.

I am fortunate to have enjoyed many lunches with Paolo, Walter and Franco, joined often by other impromptu invitees. Everyone would be welcome at their table; their generosity of spirit was remarkable. I will recount one particular occasion, as an example, but there could be countless others.

It was August, not yet eleven in the morning but already the heat hung thickly on the breathless air. Piazzale Michelangelo was still, vehicles were parked haphazardly, their drivers panting like lions in the shady angles created by open car doors. Faint tones of Verdi filtered from a car radio. Paolo waved as I walked across to the small fruit stall where he stood eating slices of watermelon, which were being cooled by a gently dripping hose pipe.

'Tobino. Com es dai?'

'Bene grazie,' I replied and switching to English, 'I have just finished the contract discussions with Renato, so I am free for the day.'

'Great.' Paolo's voice was deep. 'Let's go for lunch!'

He squeezed his big square frame into the driver's seat of his Fiat, the state of the car reflecting his complete disinterest in the "machina" that fascinates so many of his compatriots.

'It's hot. We should have some cool vernacchia at Donatello's before going to Fagioli. We need to drink some white because at lunch today, Tobino, we drink only Tegelato!'

'Tegelato, what's that?' After a few years working in Europe I'd learnt quite a lot about regional wine and food but could not connect with this name at all.

Paolo's eyebrows leapt upwards and his grin spread his black, bushy moustache across his face. 'Wait and see.'

We sped down into the city, crossing the river Arno two bridges up from the Ponte Vecchio. Ignoring the "senso unico" or "one way" signs and a few car horns, we took the street leading into Piazza St Croce and pulled up right outside Donatello's.

'Are you sure we can park here?' I asked meekly, pointing to the No Parking towaway signs.

Paolo looked at me. 'Tobino, I was born one hundred and fifty metres from this spot. I have lived here all my life, I have spilled blood for the blue of Santa Croce in the Calcio Storico. This is my patch and I park where I wish.' He opened the door of Donatello's and ushered me inside.

Donatello's was the smallest deli-cum-winebar I had ever seen. The floor dimensions were about the size of the service box on a tennis court, yet crammed into this small space was a vast range of wines and produce that could have easily filled a medium-sized supermarket. It was an oenological Tardis. Two sides were stacked floor to ceiling with wine cases and bottles, giving a "cellar library" feel. The other two sides were covered with shelves filled with dried pastas, tins, cakes, bottles of vinegar and oils of every kind. The most colourful shelves held storage jars of sweet red and yellow peppers, pickles, fruits and preserves; some contained produce that, given dark thoughts and a vivid imagination, could have been the leftovers of some ghastly Nazi experiment.

We maneuvered ourselves around a huge demi-john of olive oil that stood in the centre of the remaining space of the floor. Stepping over wooden boxes filled with more wine, we stood in front of the tiny glass deli-counter that was piled high with cheeses of all shapes and sizes, salamis, charcuterie and sausages. Without asking, Paolo reached behind the counter and took a bottle from the refrigerator. With a flourish, he opened it with a pump corkscrew that was ingeniously fixed to the wall between two hanging baskets stuffed with dried chillis.

He poured glasses, and the tang of the crisp white wine, Tuscany's only drinkable white, set my taste buds alive like swaying sea anemones suddenly springing bolt upright.

'Hello Tobino. So, Bafo, I see you haven't painted your shop doors as you said you would.'

Donatello made up for his lack of size with a sharp tongue. He balanced a plate of crumbled parmesan and a few chunks of salami on a Panatone box in front of us.

Nicknames extended to Florentines too and Paolo's "Bafo" referred to his luxuriant, black moustache.

'That's because your poofter cousin hasn't sent his painter friend to do it,' Paolo replied, replenishing wine glasses with one hand whilst popping a chunk of Reggiano in his mouth with the other.

Donatello immediately switched to Italian and the two of

them started shouting and waving arms at each other, swapping abusive remarks in a dialect I could not follow at all.

'What are they arguing about?' said Franco walking through the door, making a beeline to the fridge, helping himself to a bottle, opening it from the hidden corkscrew and replenishing glasses all in one go.

'I think they are arguing about Donatello's cousin.'

'What, the poofter?' asked Franco.

Back into English, Paolo said, 'See, Dona. My case rests; everyone knows he is gay!'

'And who cares,' Paolo whispered in my ear, 'but it's fun to wind up Dona.'

'Now calm down everyone.' Franco's lecturer's voice softened the atmosphere. He had an ability to reason from both sides of an argument that one could only demonstrate if one's day job was a lecturer in electrical engineering whilst in the evening, one ran a night club called The Red Garter. Tall and pale, Calamini could pass as a priest or an assassin. He is in fact one of the world's great gentlemen; as gracious as he is gentle. He offered his judgement. 'The only way we can resolve this is to ask Frederico himself if he is gay.'

Donatello snorted like a hippo blowing water.

Franco continued, 'He may of course deny it, but we will see the truth in his eyes.'

'Right,' said Paolo. 'Give Frederico a call, Dona, and ask him to come round for a glass to discuss the matter.'

'I can't because he is up at San Cresci, running the restaurant for a week while Gianni takes a holiday. His mama is making the pasta and Frederico is cooking.'

'Mama mia. That means the food will be good. He might shop around the corner, but he cooks like a dream. Let us drive up to

San Cresci for lunch and enquire as to the slant of his sexuality,' Franco proposed in theatrical tone.

At this point the door opened and Walter walked in. With a quick "bongiorno" he walked straight to the fridge, helped himself to a bottle of vernaccia, opened it from the cleverly hidden corkscrew and filled everyone's glass. He quaffed the glass in one, shucking his teeth against the coldness of the wine.

'Where are we going for lunch, Fagioli's?'

'No,' said Paolo. 'We are driving up to San Cresci to eat lunch. Frederico and his mother are cooking while Gianni is on holiday.'

'Excellent,' said Walter. 'He may be a poof, but he's a great cook.'

'Aaahh!' Donatello could stand no more. 'Fuck off, the lot of you and I hope he poisons you!'

Laughing, we poured out into the street and squeezed into the Fiat. Just as we were about to pull away, Donatello tapped on the window and passed two opened bottles of wine with corks put back, plastic glasses, and a half metre of thin, dried sausage.

'You will need sustenance. It will take 45 minutes to drive.'

Four men in a Fiat took the road away from Santa Croce towards Certosa. Such a simple phrase does not adequately describe the experience of driving the wrong way down one-way streets, ignoring traffic lights and most other vehicles, then cutting through a truck repair business to avoid a hold up at the crossroads. 'It's okay, Francesco is a friend of ours,' said Franco as he sensed my question.

Inside the car a debate about Tegelato wine ensued and took most of the concentration of Paolo, who was mixing the role of driver with wine expert. Consequently, our journey was interspersed with near misses and sudden steering adjustments, as he made his argument in favour of this ancient wine making technique.

Tegelato by the way, is a red wine of any grape, but in Chianti mostly sangiovese, which is sealed by an earthenware cap at the end of the bottle. The wine is then laid, in the ancient manner, under terracotta tiles on the surface of the rooftop; "tegel" meaning "tile". The intention is to take on the heat of the sun, which is claimed to enhance the peppery flavour and add to the wine's intensity. Nowadays only one or two country winemakers continue with the tradition with the odd few bottles stuck on their roofs in memory of the old days. When I did eventually try it with Paolo I found the wine tending to vinegar and not my taste at all.

Somehow, we made it up and out of the steaming city and the Fiat wound its way slowly along a road lined with cypress and pines and dappled with sunlight. With knees around our ears and elbows in each other's chests, we passed and spilled wine and munched on chunks of spicy sausage. We were following the wine road to Greve and I gazed as we passed scrub oaks, pines and tiny vine plots heavily laden with grapes ripening in the sun. Now and then olive trees hung over the road edge, the sloping hillside held firm in place by roughly built stone walls.

Turning a tight corner, Paolo braked onto an open patch of dirt. We climbed out to relieve ourselves and admire the view. Fortini was in an expansive mood as his arc of liquid relief made a rainbow in the sunlight.

'Etruscan history was written in these hills, Tobino. Over there is one of the oldest oil fattoria in the world and beyond those hills you will find Impruneta; the spiritual home of terracotta pottery.'

'All very interesting,' said Walter, 'but my stomach is rumbling. Andeamo!'

A kilometre or two after Greve in Chianti, we turned onto a rough road that became a bumpy, gravel track leading up to an ancient stone farmhouse. There were olive trees to the side and rear of the building that sat on a split-level cut into the hill, so we had to climb up a few steps to the shaded terrace at the side. From there the view extended across a deep olive grove and vine clad valley to a small hill top hamlet beyond. The late lunchtime sun glinted on a fieldworker's car windscreen in the distance. I had consumed enough wine to imagine it to be the glinting shield of an Etruscan soldier defending against the invading Roman hordes.

Simple trestle tables covered with white tablecloths stood on the terrace shaded by the cover of an ancient climbing vine intertwined with bougainvillea. One or two tables were taken, leaving at least ten available.

'Obviously no-one has heard Frederico is cooking this week,' said Walter nodding at the empty tables.

I followed Paolo as he plunged through the plastic door fronds into the dark shade of the winter restaurant area and through into the kitchen.

'Bongiorno, Bongiorno,' he boomed. 'What's for lunch?'

'Hey Santa Croce Mafiosi! Com es dai?'

Paolo, as if on rails, made a beeline for the fridge, looked in at the bottles, sniffed and then reached for a bottle of Chianti on the shelf above. He uncorked and poured glasses in a trice.

'Fredi,' he said in English, 'we have brought our friend Tobino to look at the view and eat some proper food.'

Frederico, portly, young in face but with grey hair, wiped his hands on his apron and crossed the kitchen with open arms to give me a welcome hug.

'Watch him,' said Franco, travelling on the same rails to the fridge. He sniffed at the wine inside but took a bottle of beer, opening it and savouring a long swig.

'Hah, it's thirsty work travelling to the mountains. How are you, Fredi, and what is for lunch?'

'Well, it is a pleasure to see you boys and that you have come so far. In fact, you have picked a good day to visit. We are closed tonight so we can share lunch together. I will be delighted to cook for you.'

Frederico was so disarmingly charming that the three musketeers held back on the supposed reason for visiting and let themselves be good-naturedly shooed from the kitchen by Mama. If you had told me this venerable old lady in the blue house coat was one hundred years old, I would have believed you. But she was bright and energetic and before you could say "tegelato" we were installed at a favourite table and served wine, aqua panna and olive oil, and given a mountain of crusty bread, some charcuterie and some radishes, to keep the wolf from the door.

A few minutes later, Fredi appeared with plates in each hand. One held roasted red and yellow peppers lying in green olive oil. The other was a dish of ripe figs and orange melon strewn with thin slices of prosciutto. He also balanced a small plate of lightly battered sage leaves, which exploded with flavor in my mouth when I tried them.

'Of course, he may not be gay at all,' said Paolo strangling the pepper grinder, 'and of course it doesn't matter one bit. It is just our usual silly fun. Bon appetito!'

With that the conversation changed to tourist politics and the real fear that their beloved Firenze would soon be completely overrun with tourists.

'Admittedly we make our living from tourism but there must

be some controls. You cannot move for tourists, and not just those from Europe, Australia and New Zealand, America and Japan, but soon we will have Indians, Chinese, Brazilians and, who knows, maybe Russians in future.'

'Soon all the Trattorias in Santa Croce will be gone and there will be fast food joints everywhere. We will have to travel miles for a decent lunch and this is a great one!' said Paolo.

We had no idea how prescient this conversation would be. In 2012 as I wrote this, Florence, along with most historic European cities, was completely overrun by tourists. The pleasures of visiting nowadays are found in the out-of-the-way spots that only locals know and only introduce to a select few.

The deftness of Frederico's cooking and Mama's pasta making, became clear with the primi pasta course. There were three dishes, Frederico explained, jabbing a thick finger for my benefit as he eased himself onto the bench seat and was poured some wine.

'Mama's linguine is exceptional. These vongole came up from Livorno this morning.' The flattish bowl had swirls of thin linguine in it and the tiny clams, ticking with garlic and chilli, shone like buttercups in their field of parsley.

'This tiny ravioli is stuffed with ricotta, peas and mint and this, my favourite pasta, strozzopreti, the strangled priest, must always be served with a tomato sauce. Eat up!'

Apart from slurps and murmurs of contentment the table fell strangely silent for a minute or two; it was the longest I had ever heard quiet amongst my three friends.

'Fantastico!' approved Paolo, smacking his lips and wiping his moustache with a napkin. 'More vino!'

And we were off, this time with a debate as to where the best olive oil comes from. Paolo favoured the oil from his local area, the Val de Pesa, whilst Franco was a big Fonterotuli fan. It was a constant culinary learning curve for me. In fact, a year or so later I was fortunate to join Paolo on his annual olive oil buying trip. He called it the Porcini and Olivo trail and it took three days of solid tasting, drinking and eating. I nearly exploded from the food intake; but I learnt a lot about olive oil.

Walter ended the conversation by stating, 'Everything is good in Tuscany.' Then with a big wink at us, while Fredi was building a fire of vine trimmings on the large stone grill, he said, 'Frederico, a question, when did you discover you were gay?'

Fredi burst out laughing. 'I wondered when you comedians were going to raise the subject. Dona called me earlier to tell me you were coming, and that is why I closed for the night. I knew you idiots would eat and drink all our stock!'

'And?'

'Senti... so you want to know the truth?' He walked over towards us and slowly reached under his apron, pulling out a photograph of himself and a very pretty woman, standing on that very terrace. 'Gentlemen, I give you my wife-to-be, Leonora. We will marry in October and you are all invited to the wedding lunch!'

'Ah ha! This calls for celebration!'

And celebrate we did. Over the grill, Frederico cooked two bifsteak Fiorentina, far too much for five of us, even with Paolo among us. These were pieces of the finest steak I had ever eaten. On the bone they were each about the size of an A4 piece of paper and three fingers thick. They took a while to cook and came to the table with deep, flame-blackened grill lines. When cut, the meat was deep red in the centre and was dressed only with salt and pepper, olive oil and a squeeze of lemon. Every mouthful was delicious and hinted of the vine trimmings and rosemary sprigs Fredrico had used to baste the meat. More Chianti washed the meat down.

I was fit to burst even though I had eaten about half the portions my hungry friends had consumed. Fredi liked his bifsteak too. However, I could not resist a slice of Gorgonzola and a sweet pear that Mama produced a while later.

Paolo announced we needed Grappa to fight the evening chill and help our digestion. It was now 8 pm and we had been at the table for about six hours. San Cresci was at a higher altitude than the city, but it was still shirtsleeves temperature. We tasted Grappas and then drank "Torpedi di Livorno" and by 10 o'clock Frederico's voice was reverberating around the valley as he sang and taught us his unique Tuscan drinking songs.

If you had lit a match in the Fiat as we pulled away from the waving Fredrico, we would have combusted on the spot. Franco and Walter seemed pretty relaxed with Paolo's driving as we sang more drinking songs and bumped our way back down into Firenze. We had to stop a couple of times, once for a comfort stop and an argument about who was Fiorentina's best-ever striker, the other to inspect the scratch made by a tree that Paolo swore came too close to the car.

It was well after midnight when Paolo dropped Franco and I outside the Red Garter nightclub. We went in whilst Paolo and Walter drove home—via the odd pavement, I presumed.

Feeling nicely lubricated but in fine form I followed Franco to the bar, for just one of his famous "zombie" cocktails and then became lost in a sea of bodies jumping and dancing to the Aussie rhythms of Midnight Oil and Mental as Anything. A hand pinched my bum and I turned to recognise the blonde hair and green eyes. 'Hello stranger,' she breathed in my ear. It was a great way to end to a perfect day in Florence.

There are so many tales to be told of Florentine festivities, of mediaeval football, of mushroom hunting, of countless more lunches but they can await another time. This chapter finishes on "the morning after the night before" when I walked in to Donatello's to say thank you and goodbye until next time. Paolo was already there with a glass in his hand.

'So how was yesterday?' Donatello asked.

We told of the fabulous lunch and of Frederico's happy wedding news. Finishing the tale, Paolo winked at me and said, 'Of course, he is only getting married to cover up the fact he is gay.'

We ducked as a loaf of ciabatta whizzed over our heads.

6

Morocco

The chicken stood stubbornly in the centre of the dusty road. Jonesy pulled our coach right up to it and there began a bizarre battle of wits between the driver of a twelve-metre coach and a scrawny, recalcitrant bird.

Leaving them to it, I jumped from the coach and walked fifty metres up the half-made road to the border guard post between Ceuta, a tiny part of Spain on the African coast, and Morocco.

A Customs official occupied the small booth. He was wearing Arab clothing and smoking a cigarette. He looked at me with disinterest, took the forty-two passports from me and with barely a glance stamped each one until he came to the final passport; mine. He gave me a toothy, tobacco-stained smile and said, 'Baksheesh.'

I passed him two hundred dirhams, about five bucks, through the small window. He stamped my passport, returned all the passports and slammed the window shut. Two armed guards in ill-fitting uniforms were standing under the shade of a date-palm, next to their barrier gate hut which had been painted in red and white stripes. They ignored me completely. I waved to

Jonesy, who beeped the horn and the chook flapped away. He drove the coach to the barrier as I approached the two guards with the passports and gestured to them to please open the gate.

They gave me toothy, tobacco-stained grins and said, 'Baksheesh.'

I duly gave them one hundred dirhams each. Demonstrating immense effort, as if we had asked them to dig the Corinth canal single-handedly, they discussed who should take on the task of opening the barrier. The chosen guard duly left the shade, took two steps to the barrier, and lifted it easily by its cantilever. They ignored our waves as we drove through.

'Welcome to Morocco, people,' I said to the intrigued passengers who were looking left and right and taking in their first experience of North Africa. The place was so different to the Spanish and Portuguese landscapes we had journeyed through to get to this point.

'It's a couple of hours to Chouen where we will stop for lunch and give you a chance to stretch your legs after last night's ferry crossing, which I think you will agree was an experience?'

I was referring to the teeming, overladen freight night ferry from Algeciras to Ceuta, which we had taken to cross the Straits of Gibraltar. Jonesy flicked on Crosby, Stills, Nash and Young's *Marrakesh Express*, palmed the wheel of the Big Yellow coach and we rolled, singing, onto the main road heading south. The road was clear and, in many places, recently asphalted, so we could motor along quite comfortably passing through the reddish rocky, sandy land that was occasionally dotted with palm trees and small, basic irrigated patches of maize. The Atlas Mountains were a distant purple haze.

Although Jonesy was pleased to be in Morocco, he was not ecstatic. He was happier driving expedition trucks through

Afghanistan and the Hindu Kush, or north-south through Africa. Our relatively civilized method of transport, in a modern Mercedes coach wasn't, as he would put it, hairy-arsed enough. A gravedigger and triathlete from Sydney, he was big-framed and tough. He was also an excellent driver and I was grateful for the easy way he drove and manipulated the coach from London via Paris, Bordeaux, San Sebastian, Madrid, Lisbon, Seville, and Jerez, down to Morocco. We would need his skills once we left Fez and headed for the Atlas Mountains and the pre-Sahara.

Of all the trips I was on as a Tour Leader, the Spain, Portugal and Morocco tour was my favourite. In the late seventies our Big Yellow coach and band of 18 to 35-year-old Aussies and Kiwis were unique enough to cause a stir wherever we went. On this tour the sights, activities and cities were always fascinating and threw up spontaneous challenges that were fun to resolve.

The Moroccan leg of the trip cast a particular spell on the troops. In Morocco the rhythms of the day were gentle and easygoing. Whether lazing in the lily-pools of Meski Oasis, climbing the Merzouga dunes or experiencing the bustle and havoc of Djma-el-Fnaa in Marrakech, everyone was chilled and happy to go with the flow. If plans had to change (and in North Africa forty years ago they regularly did) the response was always, 'No worries, Tobes. She'll be fine.'

Having stopped for a stroll around the blue and white town of Chouen and enjoyed lunchtime snacks of chickpea, tomato and mint stew served in tagines by the street vendors of the medina, we took the highway to the ancient city of Fez.

Once the capital of Morocco, Fez is one of the oldest and best preserved mediaeval cities in the world. Our troops were initially more concerned by the mediaeval facilities at the Royal Fez campsite, quite different than those of the Madrid campsite, for example. There was nothing regal about the place at all. However, the Moroccan chill mode was already working its magic and in no time tents were up, the billy was brewing and a dunny-scrubbing team, led by Jonesy, had cleaned "Trap one" as best they could for our group's use. Our friend Hassan arrived and soon the sweet smell of resin smoke filled the evening air.

'Okay, we're in Morocco, so let's talk drugs.'

It was the first spiel I gave on the microphone as we drove south from the border, to passengers who were unusually attentive.

'Believe it or not, the selling and smuggling of hashish is illegal in Morocco. There are very heavy penalties, particularly for foreigners. You will either have seen or heard of last year's film 'Midnight Express'. Although that is set in Turkey, it could have been set here also. And the prisons are probably worse,' I added for effect.

'Realistically, seeing as you are here in Morocco, most of you will want to try some local dope. It's a free world, so here's how you can best enjoy it safely.' The group was all ears, the only sound the background burble of the Mercedes engine.

'Rule one: Never, ever, ever bring hashish on the bus.'

'Rule two: Never, ever, ever bring hashish on the bus.'

Jonesy grabbed the mike from me. 'Rule 3: Dope. Bus. No!'

'We've got the bloody message,' said someone.

'That's great. Sorry to be so dramatic but it's necessary. Here's how it works. When we arrive at each night stop I will give you the name of someone from whom it is safe to buy. They are all up with the score and have it in small quantities for about five bucks, or two hundred dirhams. You can pay with either currency. Smoke what you buy or chuck it away and buy more next time. Never carry it with you. Finally, a message to those who are unsure about trying some; It's cool not to, don't feel pressured. Jonesy, Looby-Lou and I will never touch it. Tonight, your man is Hassan. Subject over and thanks for listening.'

The old Medina of Fez, El Bali, is the most intoxicating of city centres to explore, but to attempt to do so without a guide would be extremely unwise. Medina el-Bali is the largest car-free city centre in the world and the maze of alleyways and narrow streets is totally bewildering.

A Medina is essentially the original walled city that is now encircled by a larger city conurbation. Also built with a defensive purpose in mind, to confuse aggressors, let alone visitors, the winding streets of el-Bali can often reduce to paths of no more than a metre wide. In Fez el-Bali there are markets, mosques, a fortress, mansions, riads, shops, houses, cafes, tanneries, restaurants, craft workshops and part of the oldest continuously operating university in the world, which was founded in AD859.

The next morning Ghali was our guide to the Medina. Our group concentrated fully on following him for fear of getting lost. His knowledge was remarkable, as was his ability to dismiss the local men who were very interested in our group of mostly blonde, Aussie beach girls. Clearly, he carried some influence.

For dramatic effect the tour began at the gates of the Medina, where we climbed the many steps to rooftop level to get some perspective on the place. Ochre, brown, pink, blue and white crenellated buildings unfolded below us forming multiple rooftop levels. Minarets and towers jutted everywhere. The buildings of the ancient centre were so crammed together that we felt we could jump from roof to roof or march up and down the levels as if upon a gigantic, multi-layered Lego construction.

Our group members were fascinated, and bombarded Ghali with questions about the buildings, prayer, Islam, the role of women, schools and generally what everyday life was like in a place that was so spectacularly different to Sydney and Auckland.

'What's that awful smell?'

'Our next stop,' Ghali replied with a grin. 'Follow me.'

He led us down steps, through alleys, back up steps, along narrow stone walkways and then stopped outside a small wooden door. From his pack he pulled a huge bag, full of mint and passed a good spray of leaves to each person.

'Hold this to your nose to ease the smell. Morocco is famous for its leather, the softest in the world. Here is the oldest tannery in Fez. It is here they treat, dye and tan the skins.'

He pushed open the door and we stepped out into a small amphitheatre. We were standing on one of the higher levels and below us fell away rows and rows of stone vats holding liquids of browns, reds, vermillion and crimson. Elsewhere, hundreds of hides were hung or laid flat on great stone ledges to dry in the sun. The leather tanners, stretchers and dyers were crouched on their haunches, their hands, arms and clothes stained filthy by resin and dye. But the stench; the foul fetid, acrid, sour rasp hit the throat like teargas. Retching and holding our breath, we fell back through the door, our faces buried in bunches of mint.

After explaining the process we had just seen and allowing a few brave ones to go back for another look, Ghali announced, 'Now it is time for refreshment.'

He led us along more alleys and narrow streets, passing copper beaters and weavers. We squeezed through a gap between two buildings and emerged in a small paved square. Ghali pushed open a double door to reveal an inner courtyard tiled from floor to ceiling with blue, white and yellow ceramic tiled motifs. There was a fountain in the centre and an orange tree stood beside a wrought iron arbour. Doors led off the quadrangle leading to individual sitting areas separated by fine muslin blinds. The space was overlooked by a gallery, made of carved wood strung with hanging flower baskets of pastel shades.

We sat on kelim cushions and were served mint tea or fresh squeezed orange juice. There were bowls of dried apricots, almonds and sherbert sweets. A French-speaking waiter circulated offering slices of sweet, sticky baklava.

The group fell silent, sipping tea, listening to the dripping fountain and catching the scent of orange blossom and mimosa.

'Fucking beautiful,' announced Lofty, a big, friendly Queenslander. 'You wouldn't be dead for quids. You just wouldn't take the money.'

It was another pristine morning as we took the road south from Fez towards the eastern side of the Atlas Mountains. Our road would take us winding upwards past Boulamene then through the Gorge de Ziz to Meski Oasis, where we would camp for three nights. During our stay we would explore Erfoud, the market at Rissani and drive to the dunes at the edge of the Sarah Desert to watch the sunrise. From there our journey would take us to Todra Gorge, Marrakech, Casablanca, and past Rabat to Tangier before crossing back to Spain.

The Atlas Mountains and the peak of Jebel Ayachi loomed tall ahead as we drove the road through Gorge du Ziz and out onto the plain towards el Racchida. The landscape was predominantly red. Earth, rock and sand all reflected various hues of rouge. Interspersed along the roadside, where water could be found for irrigation, were small green plantings of date palms and bullrushes and occasionally maize. Berber families, goatherders and roadside peddlers selling cheap rugs, woven baskets and cinnamon spice all waved as our big yellow bus burbled by. The road flattened to a wide red desert plain, with seemingly no end or perspective other than nearby mountains to our west, yet nothing to the south. Then at dusk we drove over a rise and before us emerged a large grouping of trees and palms. The battered sign read "La source bleu de Meski".

Meski Oasis had for centuries been one of the resting points for traders and caravans emerging from their Sahara Desert crossings en route to the market at Rissani where the travellers would take on water and trade with the waiting merchants. Salt, spices and textiles were bought and sold as were donkeys and camels.

A stay at Meski Oasis was a truly exotic experience for our group. Tall date-palms and stands of bullrushes surrounded the campsite. Our tents were erected around large, deep pools of blue-green water fed from a natural spring that appeared to emerge from a rock wall. The pools had recently been dredged and enlarged by the French Foreign Legion, who regularly passed by on their desert manoeuvres. The larger pools were overhung by newly planted palms and there were floating lily pads drifting in the flow by the source. Lanterns were threaded through the trees and arranged alongside pathways leading to and from the battered reception-cum-shop. Dragonflies and the odd bat skimmed the surface of the pools and in the lantern light we could make out two young women in traditional dress standing in the waters to their waist.

'Zey take the waters of La Source at evening time to improve their baby making,' explained Mahjid the manager, rolling his tongue around his heavily accented, but understandable Franglais.

'We welcome you to La Source, Meski. You are our pleasured guests.' He gestured us to the long tables set by the fire where bread, olives and a dozen tagines were awaiting our arrival.

We fell on them, tugging bread and devouring the slow cooked vegetables flavoured with Raz el Hanout and cumin spice. We drank a few Heinekens from the bus but Mahjid preferred the whiskey I had brought as a gift for him.

Naturally, Mahjid was also the hash supplier and soon the warm night was full of the familiar resin sweetness. We drifted to sleep ready for the early start to see the sunrise over the Sahara.

When they arrive, the fingers of dawn's light spread quickly over the rippling sands of the pre-Sahara. Scrambling up the ridge of the dunes we waited as the pale grey light turned tangerine, then gold and we had to screw up our eyes against the brightness. Sitting on the edge of the sand dune's peak, legs dangling, our group looked as if they were balancing a great racing yacht as it leaned into the wind.

It was chilly, and we were grateful to the Berber tea sellers who miraculously emerged from nowhere to dispense strong, sweet tea from battered urns that were strapped to their backs.

'Where do they come from?' asked Bear, a particularly hirsute sheep farmer from near Dunedin, New Zealand.

I explained I had no idea how or from where they came, only to say I knew they would be there. It was remarkable how this would happen throughout Morocco. In this instance, following Mahjid's directions, we had driven for an hour south of Rissani, on a solid dirt track into the desert. We had seen no lights and in the grey pre-dawn half-light our bus was parked solitarily, with nothing but desert and dunes as far as the eye could see in every direction. However, as if by magic, with the first seconds of daylight dawning, up would pop someone offering tea or selling handicrafts or sweets.

The Berber men offered us bread and raisins to munch with

our tea. They would only accept a tiny donation. 'Feed your guests even if you have to go hungry,' is an old Arab proverb, that I always found to be true.

Although the city Arabs had become more used to tourists and their commercial possibilities, they remained hospitable and warm, whilst the Berbers and those living in the southern regions were remarkably welcoming and generous beyond belief.

We found small ways to repay their generosity. As we drove away from the dunes, heading back towards Rissani, we waved goodbye to the tea sellers, both now resplendent in t-shirts, one with a big yellow sun logo on the front, the other with the epigram, '95% water. Beer is good for you.'

After about half an hour there was a request for a "bush stop". We parked the coach in the middle of nowhere, with not a person in sight; nothing but sand and rocks.

'Guys to the right. Girls to the left.'

Two minutes later there was a scream and Jonesy and I raced to the left side of the bus to see, among the crouching ladies, two small Arab boys walking towards us holding above their heads large iguana-like lizards, coloured red and black. The boys wore huge grins on their faces and paid no attention to the ablutions; they merely wanted to show off their prehistoric-looking catch.

The market at Rissani was a blur of dusty pandemonium. Market traders bellowed their sales pitches at the passing crowds. After ensuring our girls were suitably attired, with knees and shoulders covered, Mahjid led us through the throng, past stalls selling cutlery and coloured bowls; then there were lines of knife–sharpeners, then one of textile sellers and then one of salt and spices. There were literally mountains of Berber rugs and one man was trying, it seemed unsuccessfully, to sell cheap plastic salad spinners. God only knows where he got them.

Walking beyond the "goods" sales area we came to the donkey market where upwards of two hundred donkeys were corralled in pens of twos or fours. The smell was pungent but the noise of braying donkeys and bartering Arabs was deafening. The donkey traders and buyers, dressed in robes of pale blue, white and brown, walked in groups from pen to pen, haggling, arguing and spitting. A deal was struck by the slapping of hands, a brief tête-a-tête hug, then a great shout of what sounded to me like "Tesco!"

'Time to buy our dinner,' said Mahjid. 'Leave our guests to wander the market and come with me. The women are perfectly safe here.'

Mahjid, Jonesy, Looby Lou our supercook, the most vital member of our team, and I walked back to the village centre. All the buildings were one storey, square and flat-roofed. Some were constructed of baked mud bricks whilst those of wealthier owners were made of sloppily painted breezeblocks. Here were the butcher, the baker and the candlestick maker. With a few words from Mahjid, a boy sprinted ahead of us and disappeared around the back of the butcher's shop. An ancient, teak-skinned gentleman greeted us. He wore harem pants and a string vest. His eyes and nose were like a falcon. With great solemnity he showed us to wooden chairs where we were served warm bottles of Fanta with straws to drink through.

After a few minutes, as if introducing a vaudeville act, with a shout and a grand hand gesture, Monsieur Falcon drew attention to the side of the building. Around the corner, dragging a canvas sheet came the Arab boy and another elderly gent. Lying on the canvas in full gory view lay a freshly skinned goat.

Mahjid gave us his beetlejuice grin.

'Excellent! Fresh meat.' Then he looked at a stunned Looby Lou. 'Don't worry Louise, I am chef tonight with my friends.'

We paid the amount that you would spend for four bottles of Fanta in a Manly beach café, for meat for 50 people.

Back at Meski the day unfolded like a scene from an Antonioni movie. Sunbathing, lazing antipodeans sprawled around. Some sat up to their waist in the pools, many did hand-washing in the spring water. The camp looked like a hippy caravan site, with lilos and bed rolls strewn everywhere. Slabs of Heineken beer were laid to cool under the spring and cocktails of vodka, bought in the duty–free zone of Ceuta, were mixed with fresh pomegranate and orange juice. Midnight Oil boomed from the bus tape deck.

Bear sat with Looby Loo peeling potatoes, plaintains and onions.

'Actually, he is a lovely guy,' defended Looby when I accused her of grizzly goings on under the starlit sky, 'and it's none of your business.'

I always enjoyed working with Louise. She was a fantastic cook and always ensured our troops were well fed and happy. She would also view my occasional behavioral excesses with a weary shake of the head and an exasperated "useless".

I walked over to the firepit where Jonesy was helping Mahjid with the cooking. A great fire had reduced to embers and the goat was stretched out over a large metal grid frame. This frame was attached to concrete reinforcing rods that were ingeniously rigged so the frame could be raised or lowered toward the heat. The whole contraption was very similar to the "asadors" used by the Gauchos of South America. The meat had been rubbed with salt and cumin; preserved lemons and garlic had been stuffed into pockets cut into the fleshy parts of the animal.

I stood with them as Mahjid adjusted both the height of the grill and the level in the whiskey bottle he had opened, 'pour faire la cuisine.' Jonesy and I kept him company with a slab of Heineken and words of encouragement such as, 'Get in there, Chef!' Soon the aroma of grilling meat drew a crowd of watchers. Aussies, Kiwis, Moroccans and me, the single Pom, stood around slurping beers and vodka shots and passing the odd joint. Looby Lou and Bear arrived with spuds, root veg and onions. These were mixed with a slash of spicy stock and put into a big casserole Dutch oven that sat in the embers.

The feast that night was epic. We fed our group of 40 plus all the site workers and had enough left over to offer a few plates to a German group that arrived in an expedition truck, having crossed part of the Western Sahara. Music from drums, strings and a sort of clarinet broke out and the desert night was filled with the intoxicating rhythms of North Africa, accompanied later by the passionate grunts of a Bear from Otago.

The sun was already high in the sky as we drove westwards from Meski, following the road of a thousand Kasbahs. Our des-tination was Todra Gorge, a deep-walled canyon that channeled the Todra river and the spring melt waters from the Eastern Atlas Mountains. The normal plan was to park the bus at the entrance to the Gorge, then hike the two kilometres along a riverside track to an overnight lodge called the Todra Inn. Donkeys would transport the overnight packs needed and the main luggage, tents and equipment would remain on the bus. Simple.

Pink oleander bushes marked the entrance to the Gorge and as we arrived, as if by magic, a tea seller turned up. He accepted payment for the tea but not for the ripe dates he offered around. We sipped tea and looked up at the hundred-metre high walls of the gorge. The river, unusually, was not running fast, and the level was remarkably low. It gave Jonesy an idea.

Dismissing all instructions from the office and my pleading, Jonesy decided he would drive the bus up the river bed to the Todra Inn. All the luggage and tents were manhandled from the lockers below onto the seats above to keep them dry, and Jonesy, with a couple of our blokes for company, drove the bus into the river and started up the Gorge. We trekked alongside the river as Jonesy, his face split with a manic grin, rocked and rolled the coach up the river bed, through flowing water about half a metre deep. At times the water level reached the lockers and water sloshed through the underside of the coach. Kids appeared from nowhere and clamoured to ride on the coach and so, it was with a couple of Aussies and half a dozen Berber kids on board, that Jonesy finally reached the Inn, scraped out of the river and, with a twenty-point turn, parked the bus ready for our departure the next day.

I returned to Todra Gorge about 30 years later, to find that there is now a road that follows the Gorge past the Todra Inn, right up to the town of Imihil. But I bet in 1980, Jonesy was the first and only idiot to have ever driven a bus up the Todra river.

That night, lying on the flat roof of the Inn as we gazed into the star-filled sky, with bats and night owls careering overhead, Jonesy voiced an unexpected regret for spoiling the natural beauty by driving the bus up the river. He seemed stung by the realization he might have made a monumental cock up. 'What a fuckwit I am,' he observed. 'What happens if it rains in the night?'

'It is only snow in the high mountains that will cause the river to flood.' A French-accented voice spoke from the darkness. 'It is October now, so you will be okay.'

Two faces came over to the lantern and introduced themselves as Pascal and Oriel. In the lamplight the shadows flickered on weather-beaten faces and revealed tough-skinned hands. We shared our vodka bottles and listened as in excellent, French-accented English, they described their lives as husband and wife, itinerant mountain climbers.

Now in their fifth year of constant travel, Pascal and Oriel had ditched teaching jobs, raised a little sponsorship money and had taken the plunge. They had started in Kathmandu and trekked some of the Himalayas. Then they had climbed in the Hindu Kush and Iran. 'We got out in 1978 just before the revolution that deposed the Shah,' explained Pascal. 'For the past two years we have climbed the Simiens in Ethiopia and parts of the Atlas.'

Pascal had a gift for storytelling and held us spellbound with his tales of controlled risk-taking in the mountains with his lady. There, on a rooftop in Morocco, under a million stars, we were inspired to realise that life can be what you make of it. Working nine to five is not the only option.

'He's a top bloke and his sort, Oriel's a beauty,' was how Queenslander Lofty saw the encounter.

Two days later Ghali greeted us with a wave and a flash of teeth, as we pulled up in front of the Hotel Foucauld, or the "Fuck All", as we liked to call it. He was standing on the steps of the half-tiled portico. The hotel name was picked out in an art-deco style above two intricately carved, ancient wooden doors. The building had the exotic but faded feel of the 1920s; it was somewhere Indiana Jones might stay, not grand enough for Hemingway or Fitzgerald.

We had arrived in central Marrakech and the Foucauld would provide the perfect location from which to explore the most extraordinary city on the whole trip. The Hotel was situated just three hundred metres from the renowned beating heart of the city, Djma-el-Fna square, and was within walking distance of the Koutoubia Tower and old city walls. Our troops were all excited and keen to check in and then go exploring. Marrakech's outlandish charm was further exemplified when they saw a horse-drawn 'calech' festooned with flowers, pass two men leading camels, loaded with patterned kelims, in the opposite direction.

'Let's go!' they cried.

However, filling the 30-metre gap between the coach and the hotel entrance where Ghali was standing, were about a hundred or so young Moroccan men, all pushing, shoving and clamouring to welcome our blonde female travellers and to offer them the "best guiding service" in Marrakech. Like bodyguards ushering stars through the Paparazzi, it took Jonesy, Ghali, the two Foucauld porters and me to forge a path for our girls to reach the sanctuary of the blue and white Moroccan tiled foyer of the hotel.

Our two days in Marrakech were spent either camped in the cool sanctuary of the Foucauld or making forays into the teeming world outside. With Ghali leading our group, we took to sightseeing en masse. We frog marched to the Koutoubia Tower and in the lilac dusk of a Moroccan night we climbed to a rooftop café overlooking Djma-el-Fna square to watch the action unfold in one of the great public spaces in the world.

Acrobats, storytellers and snake charmers put on their displays as tea and water sellers wandered among the crowds. People were taking camel rides and bands of musicians and dancers entertained the people who thronged the open-air cooking stalls and grill kitchens. In the background drums beat incessantly. Many of us could not resist the smells of grilling meats, hot spices and the rhythms of the music. We split into small groups, climbed down from our viewpoint and plunged into the sway of humanity.

Self-appointed guides and protectors immediately welcomed our ladies; but it was all good-natured and the atmosphere so beguiling, that it seemed the most natural thing in the world to float late into the night on a sea of North African vibrations.

Marrakech, Casablanca and Steve's café, and Rabat the capital came and went as the Big Yellow growled along the King's Highway, heading north. Our group had changed in appearance over the past weeks. They now had tanned faces and sun-bleached hair, and most had taken to wearing full Arab jelabiyahs, or cotton overshirts, Arabic headscarves or hats. Everyone jangled with bangles and bracelets, and leather sandals or thongs were the preferred footwear for those who could not take completely to bare feet. Even Jonesy had taken on a certain Moroccan style; his huge frame was covered head to toe in a striped cotton jelabiyah and on his feet he wore a pair of bright yellow baboush slippers. A gnarly shoemaker called Saleh had made them for him overnight.

'No problem. No problem. I bring tomorrow shoes and breakfast.' He grinned a toothless promise.

Sure enough there was Saleh, first thing in the morning, with a huge pair of size 14 yellow slippers in one hand, and a loaf of bread in the other.

'You beauty,' said Jonesy as he gave Saleh a generous five dollars and a pat on the back that sent him flying half way across the road.

After a few more adventures and many miles covered, it was under a sheltering sky that we rolled into Tangier, our last stop in Morocco before taking the ferry back to Spain. I loved the place and its bohemian and artistic connections and was in fine form on the microphone, telling tales of Matisse, The Stones and William Burroughs smoking hookahs at the Café Hafa or the Kasbah Club. I pointed to the Windmill on the Beach, painting visions of Ginsberg and Kerouac writing poetry with their toes in the sand and describing Francis Bacon sketching his coffee-coloured boys with white teeth.

I pointed to the bougainvillea tumbling from the old colonial houses, to the multi-coloured fishing fleet moored haphazardly in the busy port. I asked them to look at the quayside fish vendors with their vast array of every kind of sea creature, and beyond, to the fruit market flashing bright with exotic produce.

However, the greatest cheer and loudest whoops of joy exploded when I announced, 'Over there, under the red and white awning is Eric's Hamburger bar. Eric is proud of his clean toilets and he serves cold beers and the best hamburgers in North Africa. We'll have our farewell to Morocco dinner there tonight.'

7

Hopfgarten

A thousand stars lit the night sky and the fresh snow crunched beneath my feet. My breath plumed in the cold night air as I scrambled up a small bank and turned back towards Gasthof Schernthann where the warm light from the windows shone an amber glow over the alpine scene. A couple of sleighs stood nearby, the horses stamping and shimmering harness bells.

The Tyrolean idyll was somewhat marred by the row of thirty toboggans, 'rodels' in local dialect, lined up on the snow-covered pathway outside the Gasthof. Sitting two-up astride these contraptions were 60 noisy Aussie and Kiwi revellers, all well-fuelled on atomically strong Jagertee and Gluhwein. The drinks had been served, over the past hour, with amazing efficiency by Cristal, sporting her traditional Dirndl dress, whilst her husband Hans played Tyrolean songs and a few rock and roll numbers on a full-sized harp. His speciality, "Vun, Too, Sree o'clock Rock," never failed to get the place rocking with table dancing and beer chugging.

The booze and party atmosphere had eased inhibitions as

voices were shouting:

'Where's Moose and Nancy?'

'We can't go down facing each other!'

'Hey, Jimmy, no rooting on the way down!'

'It's too cold to get my jollies out!'

Raising my voice above the cacophony of Aussie foreplay, I bellowed into the night. 'Okay, people, listen up. Its "rodel" time. Follow Rod who is leading off. Keep your feet flat to brake, not heels. Weight on the left turns you left. Weight on the right turns you ...?'

'Right, you drongo!' the crowd roared in answer.

'Cool! Now remember, it's five kilometers to the bottom. It flattens out at one point, so you will have to walk about 200 metres. Then it's full on down to the Sports Hotel. Alf, Rod and Chaz will meet you at the bottom. I will come down last to check for stragglers. Follow the rodel in front, stay on the path and please take it easy. Let's go!'

With scrabbling feet, like Thelwell riders urging speed from lazy ponies, the toboggan crocodile began to move. As the momentum increased and gravity took hold the rodels swept away downhill. There was pandemonium at the first bend as they tried turning for the first time, and abuse, laughter and screams reverberated round the moonlit valley. Bodies fell in the snow, but were soon up again, sliding sideways and off again, hurtling out of control, but the snow, soft deep snow, always caught them. That's rodelling.

Nowadays mass tobogganing is deemed too dangerous for Tour Operators to arrange themselves; sensibly, guests must be accompanied by qualified people and trained paramedics. But in the early eighties matters were more relaxed. As the manager of the winter ski operation, I ran weekly toboggan nights for three consecutive winter seasons. We were lucky that no-one was seriously injured other than sprains and bruises and one broken foot; and that was a staff member on a night off.

With the rodellers safely on their way, I pushed the door of the Gasthof open and went back inside. Hans was beaming.

'Super, Simal. A great night.'

I paid him the agreed amount for the group's fun, accepted a beer, then sat down at the circular "Stammtisch" table for locals. It was set in a hand carved, wood panelled corner and through the window you could see down the mountain to the lights of Hopfgarten in the valley below. Somewhere between Gasthof Schernthann and the village, our sixty rodellers were sprawling their way downhill. It would take them about an hour, hence I had time to grab a beer and join Peter, Seppe, Helmut and Toni who were sitting at the table.

These local guys were friends, who were not only the lead ski instructors for our guests, but also served as guides for everything to do with the mountains. They were also useful part-time evening entertainers; Toni was excellent on the guitar and the other three were well versed in Tyrolean drinking games. The boys were also on hand to offer more personal services to the antipodean girls who were interested in furthering international relations with their ski instructors. In fact, such was the demand for and the regularity of, these diplomatic liaisons, one could only surmise that most Aussie and Kiwi girls had been persuaded that it was a fundamental rite of passage to bed an Austrian ski instructor before she was 30.

The boys were used to antipodean ways. 'Pat 'em on the head and their knickers fall down,' was the answer they gave when asked to explain the phenomenal success of their wooing technique.

Is it really necessary to write about sex in memoir about European travels, you may ask? Well, frankly, it's unavoidable. Whether describing the antics of Aussies and Kiwis on ski holidays or coach adventures around Europe, Russia and North Africa, sexual activity was a key component of the culture of hedonism and freedom of spirit that made the world go around for our generation.

And go around it did, with enthusiastic abandon. Even nicknames reflected this. Some of the most active or prolific of performers carried names such as "Spoof", "Wanker", "Muff", "Dog", "Horse", "Hook", "Gash" and the evocatively described "Sperm Whale" or "Spermy" to his close friends.

Because of the regularity and limitless availability, the act of union was often enhanced by the sport of enticing the unknowing, but soon willing and energetic participant into crazy and increasingly imaginative acts; but more of that later.

Do not for one moment consider the sexual activity to be a chauvinist preserve in exploitation of women. Let me tell you our female guests and staff members were willing and active participants, and often instigators of the carnal fun.

'So, Simal, a good group do you think?'

In Hopfgarten my nickname was "Simal", a Tirolean abbreviation of Simon. Elsewhere I was Tobes.

Peter grinned, and his face wrinkled like an ancient mountain man, although he was, in fact, a year younger than I. Many years of mountain life had toughened his skin. Peter was and remains to this day a remarkable skier. Being one of the youngest ever Austrians to achieve the highest level of national ski instructor, in a nation obsessed with skiing, underlines his talent.

Pete was well travelled, charming and witty but had a character flaw that drove him to search for stratospheric levels of intoxication. We all loved him but we were on our guard when his love for a drink coincided with his stubbornness, producing a state of unique behavioural meltdown.

In this state Peter would have difficulty maintaining balance. He would often be seen talking to someone and then, as if some unseen force had propelled him, would career over to the other side of the room, shake his head and career back again, often ending on his backside.

Remarkably, the only time Peter maintained equilibrium was on skis. Full of booze he would stumble from the mountain Gasthof, barely keeping upright, but then clip into his skis and fly down the mountain, carving elegant turns at the speed of light. At the bottom he would step out of his ski bindings and promptly fall over.

'Yep. It looks like a great group. Aufgehts, let's go and see how they are and if any damage has been done.'

Seppe, Toni, Helmut and Peter would always join me on toboggan night to descend the rodel path and check all was OK. They also, after the second day of ski instructing with the group, had their eyes on prospective partners for the week.

That evening the moon shone silver beams on the south facing slopes and we shot down the track; each with our own rodel. We stopped where we could see tracks had veered off the path and checked to see there were no bodies there. We had seen all sorts.

One evening we had turned a snowy corner and come upon a set of starlit buttocks thrusting rhythmically, as the recipient howled her pleasure at the waning moon. This particular evening, and dangerously, we found a girl peeing, half-naked beside her giggling friend.

'I couldn't get my ski suit down in time, so it all had to come off or I would've wet meself,' she explained in finest "Strine" whilst tottering and waving her hands as if conducting an orchestra. It took four of us to get her kit back on. Helmut, honourably, took the job of helping her down the mountain while Seppe looked after the giggler.

'I always love the ones who laugh!' he said, skidding off down the slope with his passenger laughing and cuddling his back.

The descent took Peter, Toni and me a further twenty minutes or so. It involved waking up a guy from Invercargill who had decided to take a nap, gently breaking up a couple of very advanced love trysts and persuading them to continue on, and replacing a fence post or two.

The final slope down to the Sports Hotel, where the bus waited, was pandemonium. Rod, nicknamed "Director" for his sage nature, Alf and Chaz darted about like ice-hockey goalies, at once catching, stopping, grabbing and sliding everyone to a halt.

'Thank heavens that is over until next week,' said Chaz, as he lifted the last reveller up on to the bus before Alf drove the five minutes up the road to Gasthof Schoneck.

Gasthof Schoneck is the last building you come to as you drive out of Hopfgarten-im-Brixental, en route to Kitzbuhel. The Good Ski Guide describes Hopfgarten as a 'largish village with a pretty Tyrolean centre, dominated by a striking Baroque church. There is fast access to the extensive Ski Welt lift system that links Hopfgarten, Itter, Soll, Westerndorf, Brixental, Scheffau, Ellmau and Going.' This is then followed by a brief sentence; 'Hopfgarten has a unique antipodean connection.'

This of course is a massive understatement! Aussies and Kiwis, as well as South Africans, Americans and Canadians have been visiting Hopfgarten, both in winter and summer, on big yellow buses for over 40 years. They number well into their thousands, and of those who do visit, the majority will stay at Gasthof Schoneck.

From the outside, Schoneck looks like any other large Austrian Gasthof. It has whitewashed stone walls with wooden fascias and balconies covered by a chalet-style roof. On quiet evenings and early mornings, you can hear the rushing water of the Brixentaler Ache as it races to merge with other tributaries and join the river Inn that flows from the Swiss Alps, past Innsbruck and eventually into the great River Danube.

The building has since been redeveloped and improved but in our era, the ground floor housed a well-stocked bar, and dining rooms capable of seating 120. On the two floors above there were 22 rooms that variously accommodated two to ten people (11 at a squeeze). Staff quarters were on the first floor, where four ski drivers and four kitchen staff, male or female, shared two rooms. As Manager I had a small single bedroom that doubled as the office. The barman, because of his nocturnal duty to be the last man standing, enjoyed the much-coveted benefit of being accommodated in a room across the road. A regular weekly amusement among our team was to pick who would be the first female customer to "cross the road".

On Saturday changeover days, when 100 guests left and another hundred arrived, the arriving ski drivers would enquire of Muff, the barman, 'How many crossed the road?'

Muff, whose real name is John, and who was legendary for his entertainment skills, replied early in the season; 'I do believe they were keen this week. I had to install a zebra crossing.' From then on prolific weeks were referred to as "Zebras".

Gasthof Schoneck, our home away from home, was therefore "Party Central" for the 99 nights of the ski season. There would be up to 120 guests, up to a dozen staff, and up to a dozen ski instructors, all up to a maximum of 35 years old, all up for anything. Bacchus himself might even have been surprised at the nightly goings on.

My office-cum-bedroom doubled as the ski instructor's entertainment centre of choice. I would often climb the stairs, badly in need of shuteye, only to open the door and find a fair maiden bent over the washbasin or bouncing delightedly on a lap. On occasion there would be two or three couples entwined together as if in a Hogarth etching.

About once or twice a month, Franz, a ski instructor who was also a major farmer in the region, would visit to join in the general rumpus. Raised farming, climbing and skiing the local mountains, Franz was an ox of a man. He was not particularly tall, but square and solid. Fit and strong, he was an incredible skier, ski racer and a general force of nature. The girls would flock to him.

He and I would exchange glances when the "chosen one" accepted his invitation to join him for a cuddle. He would place her tiny hand in his farm-calloused mitt and lead her slowly to my office. We could tell when matters were reaching a climax when the internal walls would begin to shake. Muff would turn the music up to full volume to drown Franz's raucous, uninhibited rutting sounds and his companion's cries of ecstasy. Guests who spent any "tempus inflagrante" with Franz would thereafter wear a wistful, beatific smile similar to the nurse who spent the night with the Polish dentist in the film "Mash".

As I have written earlier, sexual activity was not a predominantly male driven affair. The girls were equal participants, and often more imaginative. For example, Sally, the cook from our second, overflow Gasthof, Haus Marianne, shook me awake very early one morning. 'Tobes, did you hide the keys to my handcuffs?' she angrily demanded. 'I've got a boy attached to my bed and I can't get rid of him.'

I grinned sheepishly as I opened my bedside drawer and handed over the key.

'Fuckwit,' she grunted at me, the boss. 'I'll get you you!' She gave me a wink and raced off to release her bedmate and get breakfast on for her 20 guests.

Of course, Hopfgarten was not only about sex and partying. Skiing played a major part. Each day our hundred or so guests would head up the mountain in groups of about ten, with our friends the ski instructors. We catered for all abilities from absolute beginners, through intermediates and advanced, to occasionally a high level of race training.

All our guests, not matter what their ability, would be entranced by the natural beauty of North Tyrol and the sense of fun and group camaraderie generated by the ski instructors.

The locals loved us too. We worked hard to ensure we shared our business among the local suppliers. The butcher, baker, ski school, lift company, mountain gasthofs, ski hire shop, photographer and town bars all set their weekly calendar around our timetable. We learned patches of local dialect and the Hopfgartners embraced us with their Tyrolean hospitality. We also enjoyed their sense of fun and gallows humour that one always tends to find amongst mountain communities who understand the treacherous nature of snow and ice behind its sparkling beauty.

North Tyrol is predominantly a Catholic culture and they take their saints' days and festivals seriously. One of the liveliest festivals throughout the Alps is Fasching. It started as a pagan festival but has now been adapted by the Christian church as a week of carnival and general letting off steam before the austerity of Lent and the build up to Easter. Brits have "Shrove Tuesday", and the Americans "Mardi Gras", but the Alpine countries, particularly the mountain regions in Austria, Switzerland and Germany go for it big time.

As you can imagine it took little persuading to get us involved with the festivities of Fasching week and in particular, Fasching Tuesday, the designated carnival ski day. Everyone, from staff, guests and ski instructors, to drivers, friends and hangers on put on fancy dress and skied on Fasching Tuesday. The result? Mayhem.

We met in the "liftstuberl" bar at the foot of the chair lift at 9.30 in the morning. Having waved off our hundred guests and ski instructors with a promise to meet for lunch, we took breakfast of sorts. I looked around the table as we piled in to eat speck and kase brot, washed down with half litres of beer and a schnapps or two. Shirl, the big Kiwi, was dressed as a clown, with a massive red curly wig the size of a spiky beachball; the Director had borrowed the full Tyrolean national costume complete with 'lederhosen' shorts; and Milney wore an eclectic mix of girl's white ski pants, a Greek "Mykonos" jacket and top hat. Helly was a sunflower, Hanoi, as usual looking bombed from the night before, sported predominantly red stripes, and Muff was wearing a nightgown and a fetching lacy bra— 'borrowed it last night,' he explained. Superman, real name Russell, who was one of the drivers, wore the full uniform of his superhero nickname, Superman. I had on a pair of 1960s green racing ski pants and a very large rubber frog's head mask with a hole for a mouth, through which I could breathe, smoke and consume alcohol, and two eyes, through which I could see; but only straight ahead.

'Ein fur die strasse.' The Director sensibly ordered another round of beer and schnapps before he described a strange noise he heard last night, coming from the roof of Schoneck, when he returned late from Cin Cin disco.

'I couldn't work it out. Sounded like a rugby scrum all grunting and heaving. So I climbed up the fire escape and stuck my head up over the roof eaves. Fuck me, there is Muff, boofing a flower with her ski kit on, pants round her knees and she's wearing ski goggles. "Muff, what are you doing?" I asked. "G'day Director, I'm doing what all good barmen do with their best customers; I am giving her one on the house!"'

There were guffaws all round as another round of beer and schnapps was polished off and then it was time to go.

'Noch ein fur die strasse,' ordered Hanoi, who proceeded to tell the tale of our Russia training trip a couple of years earlier. One raucous evening, we had been thrown off and banned from the Af Chapman, the beautiful schooner youth hostel moored in Stockholm harbour. Hanoi described how we ended up staying the night with the two female policemen who turned up to evict us!

Finally, at about one o'clock, after a good few more "noch ein fur die strasse" and accompanying tales of derring-do, I pulled rank. 'Right guys, we are going skiing. We'll head up to Steingrube to meet the troops then ski back to Schernthann.'

'That far?' said Milney.

I was describing a brief ski journey of two lifts and a couple of kilometres of skiing. Milney, our head chef, who lived as if he was sponsored by Four Roses bourbon, was famous for having a season pass for two winters and skiing only once; from the top of the first chair lift, 100 metres to Gasthof Schernthann.

'Don't worry, you can come up on the lift and walk to Schern-thann and meet us there.'

Nowadays Hopfgarten has a modern, super-efficient gondola

system that speeds skiers to the top of the mountain in no time. In the early eighties, it was a slow, two-man chair lift that took ages—the time to smoke two fags to be exact—just to reach middle station.

And yes, you guessed it; we had our own chair lift "Mile High" club. Requiring a witness from the chair below, associate membership was awarded "in fellatio" whilst full membership was "in Coitus veram".

Subsequently there was a good deal of skullduggery whilst in the lift queue amongst aspiring members, so they could time exactly with whom they would travel on the chair. In case you are interested, there were quite a few associate members but Toni the ski instructor was the only full member.

Our colourful band arrived at the top of the chair lift and decided, as the snow conditions were perfect, to have a quick blast down to the "Foisching lift" before joining the groups at Stoagrube.

We were a group of mixed ability. The Director, Shirl, Hanoi, Helly, Alf, Chaz and myself were veterans of a few ski seasons so could get around okay. Muff and Superman were still learning the basics. With our usual lack of care for our mates, we yelled, 'follow us' and shot off down the hill. Fuelled with beer and schnapps, Muff and Superman hammered after us, only to immediately wipe out in spectacular fashion. After stopping to check they were all right, we skied down the tree-lined piste whooping and cutting great joyous arcs in the snow. It was wonderful and soon we reached the bottom and joined the queue for the lift that would return us to Stoagrube.

From the bottom of the Foisching piste looking back up the slope, you view a natural amphitheatre with pine trees lining the slopes like sentries, before you look higher to the peak of Hohe

Salve, the highest point in the area. The majestic views and great conditions meant Foisching was a very popular place to ski and on that festival day the queue to remount the lift was long and dense; a mass of pushing, bumping skiers. The German kids were worst and could only be deterred by a well-placed elbow. The queue lined up with the piste to one side and to our left side, as we queued, there was a steep, sheer slope that ran down to a ravine valley of thick pine forest. Nothing but a line of orange tape warned the queuing skiers of the dangerous drop.

Much jollity and banter ensued as we waited. Passing hip flasks and elbowing Germans we laughed with the Austrians at our fancy dress gear. Muff arrived, resplendent in his nightdress, and none too elegantly, like a baby giraffe taking its first steps, manouevred himself and skis into the crowded queue.

'Where's Superman?' we asked.

'He is still up there rescuing a lady who has fallen.' Muff made no reference to the fact that it was probably Super who had knocked her over in the first place.

'Is Superman here?' asked a little kid, speaking in perfect English.

'Yes, young fella,' Muff replied in a serious tone. 'As it's a busy day he is flying round the mountain helping people.'

'In fact, here comes Superman now!'

All eyes in the queue looked up the piste to see a lone figure in full Superman regalia, cloak flying behind him, hurtling at breakneck speed directly for the queue.

'Look at Superman!' shouted the kids.

'Woooaah,' screamed Superman, out of control. The line-up of skiers struggled and pushed to get out of his path.

It must have been a divine hand that, like Moses parting the Red Sea, arranged for the queue to part. But with that parting a small child came too close to the edge of the dangerous drop and began to topple over. He screamed, and his mother too. At that split second, totally out of control and travelling at tremendous speed, Russell, dressed as Superman, burst through the gap in the queue. He reached out to try and gain purchase on anything to save himself, and unwittingly plucked the tumbling child from the air, setting him back on the path. At the same time, he was thrown into the air. With cloak flying behind him, he flew most of the way down the slope and disappeared into the trees, trailing a cloud of snow behind him.

'That was Superman!' shouted the boy and the queue cheered. We fell about laughing so hard that we callously ignored the potential serious injury that Russell could have sustained.

A good ten minutes later, as we were still debating the best way of mounting a rescue attempt to find our mate, or what was left of him, we heard a voice. A ski was thrown from the woodland below, then another and then Superman emerged, covered head to toe in snow; he was more yeti than superhero. Raising himself with some difficulty to his full height, blowing snow from his mouth and nostrils, and throwing his cape behind him, we saw his chest raise with a huge intake of breath. With a booming voice that echoed around the slopes he cried, 'You bastards! Why didn't you catch me!'

Much later that night at Schoneck, with the carnival party in full swing, I persuaded a charming girl from Brisbane, who had asked me to dance, to leave the dancing and creep upstairs to join me in a refreshing shower. I was still dressed in my frog suit and Raylene looked fetching in a vicar's outfit. Giggling, we opened the door to the staff shower, but we were too late. In the shower, his leg in plaster up to his knee, balanced on the shower taps, was Superman with a blonde friend devouring his bar of kryptonite as if it were the last nourishment on earth.

The Vicar and I were undaunted; our lustful bonfires were well and truly alight. Thankfully my office was empty, and we tumbled in, scrabbling at our clothes.

'Have you ever made love to a frog before?'

'No, but I am about to,' said Raylene as she crawled naked on to the bed and provocatively turned around to offer her ample buttocks. I clambered up and, naked save for my frog's head, slid easily into her warmth.

As we found each other's rhythm I was jerked suddenly alert as I felt a metal click on my wrist. I pulled violently, but I was handcuffed to the bed.

My ardour was immediately dulled. Raylene jumped off the bed and I looked around through my two frog's head eyes to see Sally and Raylene laughing.

'Gotcha.' said Sally. She smiled triumphantly, put the key back in her pocket and walked out of the room.

8

Two Gentlemen in the City

I f your spirits are low, my advice is to take a boat—any boat, ship, yacht or hydrofoil—from Pireaus Harbour bound for the islands. Drink a metrio coffee, and down an ouzo before you sail, then settle back to watch the white crests on a blue roiling sea. You will see blue, white, white, blue, the Greek flag, the sailor's uniforms and you will feel the warm sunshine and the whipping wind. Breathe the sea air and imagine what possibilities lie ahead. You cannot fail but to be uplifted.

Feeling low myself one morning in June 1982, I boarded the hydrofoil to Aegina, and was met on arrival at the quay by one of two gentlemen, who to me, embody all that is gracious in Europe.

Spyro sat astride his beloved solex moped. Some might have described his features as well-worn; I preferred patrician and weathered. He greeted me in his Bryanston and Oxford accent and suggested a welcome glass at one of the waterfront bars of Aegina port. A couple of hours later, with Spyro pushing his moped, we walked the few hundred meters to his pistachio farm. The green door in the tall, whitewashed wall opened to reveal a shady garden, a one-storey stone house and a few hectares of pistachio trees. Through the trees, you could see a small wooden chalet—Spyro's living quarters. We sat on the terrace, surrounded by pots brimming with flowers and herbs. His venerable mother served us lunch of salad and baked vegetables and we drank a fresh tasting white wine.

'Will you join us in London for the end of season bash?' I asked after a long conversation, ranging from operational and contractual stuff, through the rating of our current crop of tour leaders and on to the Greek view of what civilization really means.

'I would be delighted.'

'Come a day early and we can have a lunch and catch up with Rudi Pfister.'

'My dear boy; that would be a true pleasure.'

Feeling suitably uplifted, a few hours and ouzos later I took the last hydrofoil back to Athens.

Two weeks later, continuing my tour of our European helpers, fixers and partners, with my spirits ebbing lower because of the daunting nature of all the things that had to be done, I drove in to the car park of the Pilatus Bergbahn. This was the departure point for the cable-car gondolas that glide to the summit of Mount Pilatus, Luzern.

Rudi sat astride his powerful BMW motorbike. Some might have described his features as well-worn; I preferred distin-guished and surprisingly youthful, enhanced by a tiny pony-tail. He greeted me in perfect English that had been polished en route to becoming a renowned Swiss Hotelier in Davos and now the manager of the two mountain top hotels in Luzern; Pilatus and Kulm.

Suggesting luncheon before taking the Gondola up the mountain, he offered me a helmet and I climbed onto the pillion seat. With a throaty roar, we zoomed into central Luzern and then along the lakeside for a few kilometers until we came upon a small waterside restaurant. We were shown to a reserved table at the water's edge and served perch from the lake and white wine from the Valais. We discussed hotel room prices for the forthcoming season and reviewed plans for a new lake cruise excursion. A light onshore breeze had picked up and the late afternoon sun had turned an apricot tone by the time I asked, 'Will you join us in London for the end of season knees-up? In fact, can you come a day earlier, and we will lunch with Spyro.'

'Now that would be an absolute pleasure.'

Lunch with my two friends was at the Savoy Grill. Daki Dave, my management colleague, joined Spyro, Rudi and I. Daki and I relished the opportunity to lavish hospitality upon these two gents, who had offered us so much help and advice, not to mention hospitality, over the years as we had grown from Tour Guides into Managers, or "Poachers turned Gamekeepers" as some of our Tour Guide friends surmised.

With our greeting formalities over and aperitifs in hand, we listened as Spyro explained the challenges of converting an ex-Greek naval minesweeper into the leisure cruiser that would carry our groups on Greek Island cruises the following year.

'Greek shipbuilders operate to a different timetable than everyone else. Bloody frustrating.'

'The Swiss would build it on time,' I offered.

'Yes, but what a boring boat it would be,' laughed Rudi.

'I can understand you must be tearing your hair out. But you haven't got any!' Daki had a directness that was part of his charm.

The silver trolley arrived, and everyone plumped for the beef.

Daki commandeered the wine list and decided we should invest some of the company's hard-won profits in a few bottles of decent plonk.

Rudi's eyebrows shot up as a Chateau Margaux arrived. He whispered a word in the Sommelier's ear.

'We will enjoy this one David,' he said to us, 'but I have chosen the next. I want you to have enough money left to pay my prices next year. The Sommelier here knows me from Davos. He will bring us a perfectly drinkable wine at a sensible price.'

'Boring Swiss bastard.'

Our two European gentlemen were terrific lunch company and displayed great natural wisdom and accuracy with their predictions for European tourism.

'Of course, Greece is a basket case. At some time, the economy will implode and who knows what will happen then,' said Rudi. 'You can sell cheap holidays to the Russians, Chinese and South Americans who will start arriving in their hordes. You mark my words.'

Spyro took up the thread.

'Tourism will swamp us if we are not careful, but we cannot deny people's rights to travel and be curious. Travel, I would say, is a great thing that brings us together by fostering understanding and acceptance of our cultural differences but—and it is a big but—are we to stand by and watch as Europe drowns in over-tourism?'

'More tourists mean more money for you guys,' I said.

Rudi sipped his claret and agreed with his Greek friend. 'You are missing the point, young Tobes. Many, many people will make millions from tourism. But with that opportunity comes responsibility. Whether it is Paris, Venice, Florence or London, or Base Camp Everest or the Amazon river, human beings are responsible for the upkeep of our living space, our planet. As the cruise ships grow in size and touring coaches carry more passengers, as visitors leave waste everywhere, someone has to bite the bullet and do something about it. It starts with governments but should also stretch to all who have their fingers in the tourist pie.'

'Fat chance of that.'

'You two young men have a great future in the travel business,' announced Spyro. 'You cannot change the world, but I urge you to remember this luncheon and do whatever you can to encourage the sort of travel that will not fuck up our planet.'

'Well that's all very good,' said Daki, picking up the wine list 'But this discussion is not keeping my glass full. Where's that mate of yours from Davos when we need him?'

Rudi took the wine list from him and ordered more claret.

'So who will be attending tomorrow? I do hope the Florentines will be there?'

'Yep. They have been here for a day or two already. The bastards beat us at darts last night.'

Daki was referring to our annual darts match with Paolo and the gang. We had started the challenge a couple of years previously and won easily. Defeat of course was like a red rag to a bull for our Italian mates, so any visitor to Florence in the past two years would have to avoid flying practice darts in the Leather shop, Francesco's wine bar or Walter's silver.

'And others?'

'It will be a good turn out,' I took up the thread. 'Dennis from Corfu, Tony and Pierro from Rome, Onur from Istanbul and Juan from Barcelona will all be there.'

At that point the cheese trolley arrived.

Daki, who was last to be served, loved his cheese, and the

smellier and runnier the better.

'Some of that please, and that, and definitely that one, then some of that.'

'Sir has selected some Forme d'Ambert, Salers, Epoisses and this is from Banon.' The waiter pointed to his selection.

'Absolutely marvelous, thank you,' said Daki with charm. 'Ponce,' he said under his breath when the waiter had left.

'Why don't we start wine and cheese tours?' I mused.

'Call it Fromage & Frolics, or Plonk & Parmesan.' Daki was always at his creative best after a few clarets.

'I can see your young brains are whirring,' said Spyro, elegantly folding his napkin. 'So tell me how you see the future for travel. Where will growth come from?'

I always enjoyed the chance to lunch with Spyro or Rudi. They both loved to take the role of mentor; to lead us in discussions that were more meaningful than the usual banter.

'Experiences and Activity,' I said.

'Top-end luxury,' said Daki.

'I like your thinking,' said Rudi. 'I have worked in the hospitality and tourism world for many years and I feel a change coming. Luxury will no longer be just about expense, but will be about the ability to use your precious time to do things that will enhance your life. Life experiences are what people are after.'

'Bucket lists, and I have ticked one off my list today with a Chateau Margaux!' Daki was happy. 'Let's have a digestif!'

And so our lunch faded into early evening. We managed to pay the bill with our company credit card before Spyro or Rudi did. It was always a challenge to beat the stunning generosity of all our European friends.

Today, as I write this, I clearly remember that luncheon. My mind was filled new travel ideas but also with a genuine fear for what is now happening; overtourism and travel activity that is simply unsustainable if we are going to continue to enjoy our world. As a consultant today, I work exclusively with travel companies who take their sustainable role seriously. Not enough do.

I continued to work for the company in various roles until the end of the 1980s when the urge to try something myself was too strong to deny. Maybe there is another volume to be written about further Big Yellow stories, French holiday companies and small group adventures.

Suffice to say the years I spent from 1978 until 1989 were the most formative and fun. I learnt a lot about leadership and how to make things happen. I travelled throughout Europe, Russia and North Africa. I visited Australia, New Zealand, Canada and the USA all as part of working for a remarkable travel company. I was a member of a small team who were responsible for organising trips and developing travel products for literally thousands of young Aussies and Kiwis.

Most importantly; I made friends for life.

And finally...

Most of the characters and friends in this book are now in their sixties. A few in their seventies even. Time has not dulled their enthusiasm for life nor has the sense of camaraderie faded.

It was The Director who first introduced me to the phrase, "Never spoil a good story by telling the truth." So those who were there will recognize that for sensitivity or discretion, I have changed a few names and occasionally crashed together events to make the storytelling more succinct.

There is a true bond of friendship amongst those who shared lives together working in the Big Yellow era. When we meet, often years apart, to blow the froth off a couple, it is as if nothing has changed, apart from the expanding waistlines and thinning hair.

Life has dealt us some tough cards along the way. We have lost friends early. Frankie Petersen for one, and of course, the irreplaceable Paolo Fortini, whose death has left a massive hole in all our hearts.

But the spirit lives on and in giving thanks to you all for your life-changing friendship I can only finish with, 'Let's go to lunch.'

About the author

Abandoning a career in drama, Simon Tobin has variously been a tour guide and manager, kayak instructor, ski guide, and travel entrepreneur, as well as Managing Director and Main Board Director of a large travel company. Now a business consultant and public speaker, Simon lives in Austria. When he's not skiing, golfing or hiking, he spends his time helping small UK travel businesses to grow, and teaching Business English. Find him at www.tobins-consulting.com

9 783950 469707